Editing
Historical Records

Editing
Historical Records

P. D. A. Harvey

THE BRITISH LIBRARY

Dedicated to the Chairman and members of the Advisory Board of the
Portsmouth Record Series

© P. D A Harvey 2001

First published 2001 by
The British Library
96 Euston Road
St Pancras
London NW1 2DB

British Library Cataloguing in Publication Data
A CIP Record is available from The British Library

ISBN 0 7123 4684 8

P. D A Harvey has asserted his right under the Copyright, Designs and Patents Act 1988
to be identified as the author of this work

Designed and typeset by Geoff Green Book Design
Printed in England
by St Edmundsbury Press, Bury St Edmunds

Contents

Acknowledgments

Of my many debts of gratitude to those who have contributed to this book the latest is to Professor Mark Greengrass and his colleagues who in the course of a day that was as enjoyable as it was instructive showed me the work of the Humanities Research Institute at the University of Sheffield. I am grateful too to Dr David Crook, Dr A.I. Doyle, Dr E.M. Hallam Smith and Mr David Way, who have all read part or all of the draft text; the finished book is much the better for their comments, corrections and suggestions.

In writing that draft, however, I was drawing on what I have learned from so many people over so many years that it is impossible to offer adequate acknowledgment. Outstanding among them are the editors of the texts that have passed through my hands as General Editor, first of the Southampton Records Series, then of the Portsmouth Record Series; it has been a pleasure and a privilege to work with every one of them and they have all taught me far more than they can possibly have realised. I would say exactly the same of the Technical Advisers to the Portsmouth series – the late Mr S.G. Kerry, Mr G.F. Tucker and now Mr Brian Iles – and of the past and present members of its Advisory Board as well as of its earlier Advisory Panel and Editorial Board. I greatly appreciate the friendly encouragement in writing this book that I have had, since it was first mooted, from all members of the Board, especially from the late Professor R.B. Wernham, even if I have not followed to the letter his sensible advice: 'Never mind about footnotes and things – just write what you know'. Above all I am deeply grateful for the unfailing support and help that I have had in all matters from successive Chairmen: the late Dr Dorothy Dymond CBE, the late Councillor E.H. Taplin and Councillor F.A.J. Emery-Wallis CBE.

My wife, Yvonne Harvey, has not only read the whole text, eliminating many infelicities, but – an even greater contribution – has uncomplainingly lived with an endless sequence of edited records throughout more than thirty years of marriage.

P.D.A.H.

List of illustrations

Abbreviations

BRA	British Records Association
Brit.Ac., RSEH	British Academy, Records of Social and Economic History
Man.Rec.Cux.	*Manorial Records of Cuxham, Oxfordshire, circa 1200–1359*, ed. P.D.A. Harvey (Oxfordshire Record Society, 50; Historical Manuscripts Commission, Joint Publications, 23; 1976)
PRO	Public Record Office
PthRS	Portsmouth Record Series. The title etc. of each volume is given in Appendix 1.

1

The rationale

This book and its background

This book is about editing documentary texts. It is not, however, a manual to the conventions to be followed by an editor. It does not set out detailed rules for dealing with medieval abbreviations, bizarre seventeenth-century spelling, illegible Victorian handwriting, or any of the other minutiae that make an editor's work so trying – and so fascinating. There are other works that do this more than adequately and I would particularly mention the two books by Dr R.F. Hunnisett that together are rightly seen as the record editor's *vademecum*: *Indexing for Editors* (1972) and *Editing Records for Publication* (1977).[1] The present book is not trying to compete with these works, still less to replace them.

It will, however, look at the principles underlying these rules and at the considerations the editor ought to bear in mind when adopting them. It is essentially a book about the strategies of editing and although it will look, even closely, at possible tactics this will be in the context of their broader implications, their part in the strategies. Dr Hunnisett also starts from the strategies, and much of what I say may be seen as an expanded commentary on his invaluable chapter on 'The initial decisions' – in nearly everything I entirely agree with him. These principles and strategies need constant reiteration, constant rethinking, and that there is a need for this book I am in no doubt: it is all too easy to embark on editing as a mere mechanical exercise, a relaxing adjunct to the stern work of writing history. It is not, and viewing it in this light, without sufficient thought about its objectives and the best methods for achieving them, does no service to historical scholarship.

It is a highly personal book, and by way of underlining this I have not hesitated to use the first person singular in writing it. It is offered as the result of work in editing documents over many years and of much thought on what is involved, how best to do it. Footnotes and references will be kept to a minimum: the book is the product of experience, not the product of research. My first essay in editing – indeed, my first

1   BRA, Archives and the User, 2 and 4.

published article – was an account of the Great Fire of London in 1666, written in German and extracted by a later copyist from the autobiography of Franciscus Rapicani, who was accompanying a Swedish embassy in London at the time. The recent discovery of the original manuscript autobiography has revealed almost text-book demonstrations both of the difficulty of accurate transcription – the late-nineteenth-century copyist had found the early-eighteenth-century hand harder to read than I had realised and had made mistakes – and of misplaced editorial ingenuity in solving the non-existent problems that resulted.[2]

My second editing project was on an altogether different scale: 700 pages of Latin text, records of an extraordinarily well-documented Oxfordshire village between 1200 and 1359.[3] Here I came up against some of the difficult problems that can confront an editor – difficult but common. I discovered how, if one is to present a text drawn up in successive stages, one writer commenting on what another had written, the editor must carefully distinguish the contribution of each hand if the document is to be understood at all. I discovered how, if one is to make any attempt at extending correctly the abbreviations in records such as these, it is not enough to take into account contemporary orthography – one must also try to establish the detectable idiosyncrasies of the individual writers. I discovered too how easy it is for an editor to ride roughshod over points of this sort, thereby seriously diminishing the value of the work.

This volume of manorial records was completed in 1972 and published in 1976. In the same year I sent to press a book of reproductions of medieval local maps, with essays by specialists on each area; it printed the maps' inscriptions and a few closely related documents, and brought home to me how difficult it can be to devise consistent rules for transcribing even very short passages that cover a long date-span, in this case from the mid-twelfth century to the end of the fifteenth.[4] Meanwhile I had become a general editor of two series of record publications. Between 1966 and 1978, as joint general editor of the Southampton Records Series, I was responsible for seeing three volumes through the press.[5] Then, in 1969 Portsmouth City Council, following the success of the Portsmouth Papers, pamphlets on particular aspects of the

---

2   P.D.A. Harvey, 'A foreign visitor's account of the Great Fire, 1666', *Transactions of the London and Middlesex Archaeological Society*, 20 (1959–61), pp.76–87. The full original manuscript has now been published by E. Bachmann, 'Die Lebensbeschreibung des Franciscus Rapicani (1636–1721)', *Rotenburger Schriften*, 82/83 (1995), pp.151–224.

3   *Manorial Records of Cuxham, Oxfordshire, circa 1200-1359*, ed. P.D.A. Harvey (Oxfordshire Record Society, 50; Historical Manuscripts Commission, Joint Publications, 23; 1976).

4   *Local Maps and Plans from Medieval England*, ed. R.A. Skelton and P.D.A. Harvey (Oxford, 1986).

5   Vols 13, 15 and 17 in the Series, respectively *The Admiralty Court Book of Southampton, 1566-1585*, ed. E. Welch (1968); *The Southampton Terrier of 1454*, ed. L.A. Burgess (1976); *The Beaulieu Cartulary*, ed. S.F. Hockey (1974).

city's past, scholarly but with broad appeal, decided to launch the Portsmouth Record Series, editions of documents for the history of the city and the surrounding area. I was invited to become its general editor, and thirty years later, with the tenth volume about to go to press, I am still in post, albeit having moved my home from Southampton to Durham in 1979.[6]

There is nothing in the Portsmouth Record Series that has not been carefully thought about, from the choice of documents to be edited to the position of every comma. This is not to say there is nothing wrong, that no mistakes have been made; but where this has happened it is the result of conscious decision, not of sheer chance, the mood of the day or the whim of the printer. The first meetings of the Editorial Board of the Series were virtually seminars on the whole philosophy of publishing historical records, as we discussed why we should do it at all, what our objectives should be and what strategies, what methods we ought to adopt. In thus starting from first principles we hoped, ambitiously and perhaps arrogantly, that we might 'help to set a new pattern for the publication of local records in Great Britain' – words that appear in each volume in the Series. In one respect at least the Series broke new ground from the start. The City Council wanted books it could be proud of, in achieving the highest national and international standards not only of scholarship but also of book production, books aesthetically pleasing that the city's Lord Mayor could properly present to visiting dignitaries. The design of the first volume, setting the pattern for the Series as a whole, was by Stanley Kerry, and it is a measure of his success that it was included in the National Book League's exhibition of British Book Production in 1972 – a most unusual distinction for a volume of local records. I have more to say later on the part good design and layout can play in presenting historical texts: the advice that a skilled book designer can give is immensely helpful in problems of editing that at first sight have little to do with printing – and I myself, the works published in the Series and this book all owe a great deal to Stanley Kerry and to his successors as Technical Adviser and Art Editor to the Series, Mr G.F. Tucker and Mr Brian Iles. For the way the records were presented, for the style and methods of editing in every detail, I was from the start given full responsibility by the Editorial Board and its successors, with much encouragement and with extremely helpful advice when it was sought. I have been able to follow through my own ideas on editing records, to experiment even, which has made the work for the Series exceptionally rewarding.

A great deal of what follows is based on my work for the Portsmouth Record Series – often explicitly. It represents a significant part of my working life and professional output, presenting a wonderful opportunity to meet the documents, the problems and the historians of a wide range of topics and periods, from twelfth-

6   The volumes published in the Series are listed in Appendix 1.

century royal and private charters to records of adult education in the twentieth century. Every volume has been given the same thought and care that went into the inception of the Series. This, with the heavy copy-editing that resulted, has made it impossible to achieve the annual publication that has been the aim of most record-publishing societies; on average the Series has published one volume every three years. That some other record-publishing bodies have moved to a similar pattern is, I believe, a measure of increasing care in production, not simply of financial constraint. But even the most careful thought does not always produce the right answer; with hindsight there are some decisions on which I have reservations, things I would do differently another time, and I shall try to look critically at all we have done, seeing the drawbacks as well as the advantages. And while I am bound to draw heavily on my experience with the Portsmouth Record Series, I am well aware that in some ways record publication for an entire county or other wider area, or for the country as a whole on a thematic or other basis, poses other, different, problems. I have tried to take this into account in looking widely at record publication in general.

Though I have not looked beyond England and Wales for my examples, all I say applies equally to record publishing in Scotland and Ireland. Some applies to record publishing on the Continent, but rather less, since in some countries there is a tradition of training historians rather more extensively in editorial methods and in the management of archival sources, whether in the record office or in print. I have taken into account only archival texts, documents that were originally written to serve a functional purpose, legal, administrative or whatever. Other texts – narrative, religious, scientific, literary – pose the editor many of the same problems as record texts, and much that is written here applies to them too. However, they also raise problems that seldom if ever occur with records. Among them are how to establish the text as originally written, sometimes from the starting-point of many late and corrupt copies with complex interrelationships; how to spot and identify phrases, sentences or long passages taken over from other writers; the frequent need for full and elaborate annotation. These and other problems peculiar to these non-record texts are simply ignored here: record texts pose quite enough problems peculiar to themselves.

The advent of electronic publishing, with all the advantages it can bring, might seem to make this book not so much unnecessary as outdated before it was even written. There can be no question that electronic publication offers immense opportunities for radical changes in the way historical records are presented to the user. It may well, for instance, become the norm to make a transcribed text available on the screen alongside a digitised image of the original document – indeed, this seems a reasonable, proper and likely development. In this case some issues discussed below in chapter 3 will vanish: if the original document is instantly accessible to the reader, there will be no need to agonise over the finer nuances of transcription as every detail will be there, more precisely and more fully than could ever be achieved through typography, though the need for simple accuracy in reading and transcription will be undiminished.

On the other hand, whatever techniques are available, practice is often a long time catching up with them, and there are likely to be many volumes printed in traditional form before the publication of historical documents is finally swept into the electronic revolution. Despite its extraordinary development in the past fifteen years, electronic communication is still in its infancy, scarcely beyond the threshold of realising its potential. Although we can make good guesses, we cannot be certain what form or forms will come to be generally accepted for record publication. Indeed, the technology is at present moving so fast that universal standards are only emerging, though Standard Generalized Mark-Up Language (SGML) has now gained wide acceptance for texts in the humanities. Nor can we be sure which technical features are likely to be long-lived, which transient, undergoing continuing radical change. This affects the means of transmission, the delivery platform: is the compact disk here to stay or is it a passing phase? It affects the compatibility between systems, essential for efficient linkage and searching, currently achieved by devices that are, at best, cumbersome. It affects marketing: even a non-profit-making publishing body has expenses that need to be recouped, making it harder for it to offer simple Internet access to its publications. Above all, it affects the preservation strategies: how is the permanence of the electronic data to be assured for certain, no matter what developments occur in hardware or software? All these questions will be solved, perhaps very quickly. But even if electronic publication soon becomes the norm, much of this book is as relevant to publication on screen as to traditional print and in any case it could well be helpful to have on record a discussion of the state of the art in the last phase of the traditional medium. It may even serve as a point of reference for whatever changes come to pass.

Historians and records

The first question discussed by the board of the Portsmouth Record Series in 1969 was, why do it at all? Electronic publishing was then in the unforeseen future, but the growth of the local archives network and the development of cheap photocopying and microfilms meant that the vast majority of English historical records were now accessible to reference and research in a way they had never been before. '"Copy records while you may" is a good motto', wrote H.E. Salter in his introduction to the Boarstall cartulary in 1930; 'they may soon be lost or pass into the hands of an owner who is illiberal'.[7] Neither risk had been wholly eliminated forty years later – nor yet

---

7   *The Boarstall Cartulary*, ed. H.E. Salter (Oxford Historical Society, old series 88; 1930), p.xi.

today – but both were vastly diminished. However, despite these considerations the board was quite clear that there was still a role, and an important role, for publishing historical records. The developments that had made records so easily available had to be taken fully into account in deciding just what was to be published and in what form. But that publication was as valuable as it had ever been – to amateur and professional historian alike – there was no doubt.

This is not the place to discuss the use made of record texts by historians of every sort – from those who write the history of a single family or building to those who write the history of the nation. It is now fully accepted that archival records, documents created for a functional purpose at the time they were written, are crucial to almost all historical writing. Nor is this the place for a detailed account of how this came about, the extraordinarily interesting interaction of historical and antiquarian research that led, over the centuries, to the development of historical writing as we understand it today. However, a brief look at some of the ways record texts have been used and presented in the past is helpful to our understanding of the different ways these records may be published and to seeing what issues are involved in choosing between them.

Certainly not just drawing on archival texts as a source of information but actually transcribing and publishing them is embedded deep in the tradition of English historiography. Bede, writing his ecclesiastical history in the years before 731, tells how Nothelm, a London priest, 'went to Rome and got permission from the present Pope Gregory [II] to search through the archives of the holy Roman church and there found some letters of St. Gregory and of other popes'; 'he brought them to us on his return to be included in our *History*'. These were presumably copies made by Nothelm of copies preserved at Rome after the original letters had been sent, and Bede did indeed include them in his history, quoting from some and reproducing the full texts of others, such as the letter of Gregory the Great to Augustine of Canterbury in 601, sending him the pallium of archiepiscopal authority.[8]

With this precedent later chroniclers did not hesitate to include in their works the full texts of documents they judged especially important. They might be important in the history of the chronicler's own monastery, like the letters of 1204 which refused Evesham Abbey exemption from the bishop of Worcester's jurisdiction but gave the abbey ecclesiastical authority in the Vale of Evesham.[9] Or they might be important in a national or wider context, like the college of cardinals' letter to the emperor on the election of Pope Urban VI in 1378, which Henry Knighton included

8   *Bede's Ecclesiastical History of the English People*, ed. B. Colgrave and R.A.B. Mynors (Oxford, 1969), pp.4–5, 104–7.
9   *Chronicon abbatiae de Evesham*, ed. W.D. Macray (Rolls Series; 1863), pp.132–7.

in his chronicle.[10] Thomas Elmham, chronicler of St Augustine's Abbey, Canterbury, in the early fifteenth century, went further: he drew facsimiles, including the seals, of some of the charters he transcribed.[11] All these are from the middle ages, but they are merely early examples of a custom that has continued down to the present, both among historians who write of the past and those who narrate the events of their own time – William Dugdale's *Short View of the Late Troubles* and Winston Churchill's history of the Second World War are two widely spaced examples of contemporary histories that quote many documents in full.[12]

In all these cases the documents are used to confirm the narrative and to add further detail. Sometimes their length or complexity means that they would be an interruption if inserted in the text, so they are collected together at the end; we are all familiar with historical works that have an appendix of documents, *pièces justificatives*. Here too there is early precedent: the *Liber Additamentorum* that Matthew Paris in the mid-thirteenth century produced as a supplement to his *Chronica Majora* served just this purpose, with references to it from the narrative text.[13] This was – and is – a way of keeping the documents subordinate to the main narrative. But sometimes the documents were – and are – taken as the basis of the whole work: they are allowed to tell the whole story themselves, with the help of connecting passages of narrative or explanation. In the twelfth century Abingdon Abbey produced what is sometimes called a chronicle, sometimes a cartulary: copies of the charters making royal and other grants to the abbey, held together with brief historical notes.[14] Much later and much more familiar examples of the same technique are the volumes of constitutional documents that until recently were a staple part of undergraduate history courses in English universities: Stubbs, *Select Charters and Other Illustrations of English Constitutional History*; Prothero, *Statutes and Constitutional Documents;* Costin and Watson, *The Law and the Working of the Constitution;* and others.

In works like these, from the Abingdon Chronicle to Costin and Watson, we are moving towards the idea of presenting documents not just as key evidence of the development that is the theme of the particular book, but also for general reference: they can easily be turned to for a particular text, irrespective of the text's role in that development. Collections of past records that were drawn up solely for general

10 *Knighton's Chronicle 1337–1396*, ed. G.H. Martin (Oxford, 1995), pp.202–7.

11 M. Hunter, 'The facsimiles in Thomas Elmham's history of St. Augustine's, Canterbury', *The Library*, 5th series 28 (1973), pp.215–20; A. Gransden, *Historical Writing in England* (London, 2v., 1974–82), ii, pp.350–4.

12 W. Dugdale, *A Short View of the Late Troubles in England* (London, 1681); W.S. Churchill, *The Second World War* (London, 6v., 1948–54).

13 R. Vaughan, *Matthew Paris* (Cambridge, 1958), pp.65–71.

14 *Chronicon monasterii de Abingdon*, ed. J. Stevenson (Rolls Series; 2v., 1858).

reference were for long produced purely for practical purposes. The cartularies into which medieval monasteries and other property owners copied their deeds from the eleventh century onwards served as handy compilations for rapid reference in questions of administration or dispute, and also as safeguards in case of damage or loss. The collections of statutes and year books, which survive in innumerable manuscripts of the fourteenth and fifteenth centuries and of which again there were many printed editions from the 1480s onwards – they were the earliest record texts to be printed in England – owed their popularity to their obvious practical value to lawyers.

Less obviously, the practical needs of rights of property, quite as much as historical interest, underlay the late-eighteenth-century works that mark the start of the continuous history of more general record publications in England. It would be too much of a digression to do more than mention here the relationship between the antiquarian scholarship of the seventeenth and eighteenth centuries and the law – especially the law of property – though it is relevant and of great interest. It was the great jurist William Blackstone who produced in 1759 a definitive edition of Magna Carta and related texts, while many landed proprietors would see implications for their own estates when Abraham Farley's edition of Domesday Book was published in 1783.[15] The texts published by the Record Commission from 1802 to 1848 included at an early stage what is still the standard eleven-volume edition of the statutes of the realm down to 1714 but ended with what was to have been the first volume of an ambitious comprehensive collection of materials for the history of Britain down to 1509.[16] It was now, in the first half of the nineteenth century, that historical interest replaced practical value as the mainspring of record publication. Before the nineteenth century even record publications unconnected with rights of property were likely to have more implications for practical affairs than the same works would today: the twenty volumes of Thomas Rymer's *Foedera* (1704–35) will have had some relevance to government policies of his own age, the four volumes of David Wilkins's *Concilia* (1737) to the thought and structure of the Church of England.

These different ways of presenting the record sources of history – embedded in narrative, or as a collection of supporting documents, or as a series brought together to expound a single theme, or as a work of general reference – thus all have rather different origins and development. At the same time, one way or another they all achieve the single end of reproducing the record and, looking at the ways historians present their record sources today, we can see them as points on a single, rather

---

15   *The Great Charter and Charter of the Forest, with Other Authentic Instruments*, ed. W. Blackstone (Oxford, 1759); *Domesday Book, seu liber censualis*, [ed. A. Farley] (2v., 1783).

16   *The Statutes of the Realm*, [ed. A. Luders et al.] (11v., 1810-28); *Monumenta historica Britannica*, ed. H. Petrie (1848).

wider, spectrum. At one end is the extracted passage or very short document quoted in a footnote to support or illustrate a statement made in the text. Or, if it is a longer document, perhaps relevant to more than one point in the book, it may be printed in full in an appendix, perhaps with other documents – or the documents may start to take on a life of their own in a separate volume or, indeed, a separate publication of nothing but records but still simply *pièces justificatives*, selected to illustrate and corroborate what the historian has written. Or, as we have seen, the documents may effectively take the place of narrative, being chosen to tell the story themselves, with linking passages or comments. Finally we have the book which prints the records for their own sake, and in which any commentary is strictly subordinate to them in an historical introduction. At each stage along this spectrum more and more prominence is given to the actual documents.

Looking at this spectrum we can see that different modes of presentation are appropriate to different points along it. Thus the short document or extract in a footnote is there for the single purpose of supporting what the author has written in the text and provided it does this, adequately and accurately, it is doing all that is required of it. Thus to note, say, an alteration or erasure in the manuscript, irrelevant in this context, is not only pointless but may needlessly distract the reader, and though the author may decide to retain the manuscript's punctuation and spelling in order to present something of the character of the original, it would be no less proper to decide that they should be normalised for ease of reading. A series of documents to illustrate a single theme has a wider but still limited function. Here again, though it is both proper and desirable to simplify the presentation as far as possible, the editor is more likely to retain the original spellings, note alterations to the manuscript, and so on. The fact is that our spectrum is also a scale of objectivity: the further we move along it from footnote to full edition, the more independent the documents become of the particular statement, the particular contention or the particular theme of the author who presents them and the more they take on a life of their own, printed simply for their own sake.

Historian or archivist?

This being so, how should we present the documents in a full edition? Much of a historian's training is directed towards the rigorous selection of evidence, to deciding what is or is not relevant to a particular theme or argument, often, especially for modern and contemporary historians, from vast mountains of available documents. What then could be more natural for the historian of any period, when setting about producing a free-standing edition of historical texts, than to apply the same tests of relevance that we have seen are appropriate when presenting documents focused on a particular connected theme or argument? It was on this basis that there developed, in the late nineteenth century, what we might call the all-for-history style of editing texts. The punctuation of a text, its use of capital letters, running corrections made in writing the manuscript – these and other minutiae were considered irrelevant to the use of the text by historians, that is, for the sake of the information it expressly conveys: ease of reading and ease of access to the historical content were deemed consistently more important than recording every jot and tittle of the manuscript. We see this approach in action in the Rolls Series, which included record texts as well as literary and narratives from the middle ages, and, until quite recently, in many volumes of the successive Camden Series of texts of all periods. On the other hand, the reports of two committees on editing historical documents in 1923 and 1924 recommended a closer attention to minutiae than many historical editors at that time were accustomed to, while accepting some degree of normalising: 'In punctuation it is usually considered convenient to adopt the modern practice'.[17]

The view that historical documents are edited for historians, so that any aspect of the manuscript that could not conceivably be relevant in historical research and writing can safely be simplified or ignored, is a perfectly possible approach to editing. Many notable editions of important texts have been published on this basis. But it is a seriously limiting approach, for it means that the edition, on which a great deal of time, care and money will have been lavished, is of no value to some of those who might reasonably have expected to make use of it. The point is made, indirectly, by R.E. Latham in the introduction to his *Revised Medieval Latin Word-List*; the printed texts of records, which must be a basic source for the lexicographer of the Latin used in medieval Britain, have often been edited with only historians in mind. Consequently, as long as the meaning of the text was entirely clear there was no need to take a great deal of trouble over etymological niceties, and as a result, in Latham's words,

> Of the sources available in print, few have been edited with anything like the care normally expended on Classical or even Middle English texts. Some texts abound in verbal monstrosities or conundrums, either left without comment or annotated with an erudite ingenuity that evokes admiration rather than confidence.[18]

It seems a pity that so obvious a scholarly need as this should have been so badly served by so many printed editions.

But even on its own terms, tailoring a text to meet the needs of historians carries serious risks. What seems unimportant, irrelevant even, to one generation or

---

17   'Report on editing historical documents', *Bulletin of the Institute of Historical Research*, 1 (1923–4), pp.6–25; 'Report on editing modern historical documents', *ibid.*, 3 (1925–6), pp.13–26. There is much wisdom in both reports, and they are by no means outdated.

18   *Revised Medieval Latin Word-List from British and Irish Sources*, ed. R.E. Latham (London, 1965), p.ix.

group of historians may look quite different to another. Manorial accounts of the fourteenth century provide a neat example of this – in case it seems that this first chapter is heavily weighted towards the middle ages I should add an assurance that balance will be restored in the rest of the book. It was only with the work of J.S. Drew in 1947 that the full significance of these accounts came to be generally understood.[19] Most are not just classified lists of money received and spent, of corn and livestock produced, bought or sold: they are dialogues between the official rendering the account and the lord's auditor, who would strike out items of disallowed expenditure, alter the amounts of sales and purchases and make other changes, sometimes with a word of explanation, often without, all to bring the account into line with what he considered ought to have happened instead of what the local official claimed had actually occurred. All these changes – the altered amounts, the deleted entries – are of great interest to the local historian, to the historian of prices and economic change, to the historian of estate management and to many others. But before 1947 editors of these texts saw them as running corrections by the clerk writing the account, slips of the pen instantly set right and of no historical interest, and they often ignored them altogether. In some cases an edition even includes the auditor's note explaining why an item has been changed, without mentioning that any alteration has been made – creating a nonsense. All this drastically reduces the value of these editions, which at best leave much of the story untold and at worst positively mislead. Only the few editors who meticulously recorded all these changes – probably without appreciating their significance – produced texts that are still acceptable today.[20]

In my view a vastly better approach is to try to make the edition of value to any conceivable future enquiry, bearing in mind not only every kind of historian, professional or amateur, but scholars from other disciplines and general enquirers of every kind. There should not, in other words, be one way of editing a text for the literary scholar, another way for the etymologist, another way for the family historian; a proper edition should be adequate for them all, and for many others besides. The editor of historical records is likely to be an historian, but must try to forget all the historical training that concentrates on selection of facts and their relevance to any particular topic or field of enquiry, and should instead adopt the outlook of the archivist, with the task simply of making facts available without questioning why or to whom these facts may be useful. Indeed, the editor is an archivist rather than an

---

19   J.S. Drew, 'Manorial accounts of St. Swithun's Priory, Winchester', *English Historical Review*, 62 (1947), pp.20–41.

20   An edition of these documents that ignores these alterations is F.M. Page, *The Estates of Crowland Abbey* (Cambridge, 1934), pp.226–79; one published before 1947 that notes all changes is *Surrey Manorial Records*, ed. H.M. Briggs (Surrey Record Society, 15; 1935).

historian, for the edition makes available the raw material for research, just as the archivist makes available the documents themselves. We have seen the edition of historical records at the end of a spectrum that began with the extract quoted in a footnote, but it may be more helpful to see it at the end of a different spectrum, the archivist's rather than the historian's. This spectrum has at the other end the one-line entry in a repository's accessions register or other summary list, moving successively to more detailed catalogue descriptions with full indexing, then to the calendar that is a near approach to a full edition. We shall look further at this spectrum in the next chapter.

Following this approach, the approach of the archivist rather than the historian, the editor should intervene between the manuscript and the printed page as little as possible; even where a manuscript's spelling, punctuation, use of capital letters or the like make the text a difficult one, any concession to readability should be minimal and introduced only in extreme cases. This may make the task of an editor sound easy – a mechanical, all but mindless activity. It is anything but. Stanley Kerry, the first Technical Adviser to the Portsmouth Record Series, who was a senior lecturer in printing at the city's College of Art and Design, once told me that he always warned his pupils that they must develop a thick skin against any complaints that they were being pernickety: being pernickety is what good typography is all about. Exactly the same can be said of editing. Good editing consists of pernicketiness. Anyone who is not prepared to be pernickety, not prepared to spend what might seem disproportionate time and effort on this or that minute detail, will never be an adequate editor.

But beyond this, good editing calls for erudition, intellectual rigour and consistency. These skills overlap, but do not exactly coincide with, those needed for writing the monographs that are traditionally regarded as the highest form of historical scholarship. Because of this, British universities have often had reservations and doubts over the propriety of admitting scholarly editions of historical texts as a valid exercise for a postgraduate degree, though there are increasing signs of a change of view on this and there have long been notable exceptions – several of the texts published by the Pipe Roll Society, for instance, started life as theses at the University of Reading. In fact an edited text accompanied by an historical introduction calls for a wider range of skills than the monograph alone, though in assessing it the same technical expertise should be required of the editing as of the exegesis – supervisors and examiners are sometimes less concerned, and less experienced, with the varying methods and standards that may be applied to editorial work. Certainly an edited text may be seen as a means to an end rather than as an end in itself – it opens the door and provides the material for the future research of others. But this is no ignoble or inadequate purpose, and very little knowledge and thought is needed to show that a good edition will stand the test of time, will be known, consulted and relied on by future generations of historians by whom most monographs published at the same time will be unread and forgotten. This is another point we shall return to.

Nothing in this chapter, and very little anywhere else in this book, should be seen as laying down rules. There are only three rules that must be observed in editing historical records and they can be simply stated:

1 Be accurate;
2 Say what you are going to do and do it;
3 Give full references to the document and describe it.

I shall have more to say of them in the chapters that follow and of much else too, but they are all that really matters – all else is style. Of course there is good style, there is better style, and there is less good style, and I see no reason not to offer my own views on this. But in principle I am concerned only to look at the different ways editing can be done, the various possible answers to the questions that will arise, and the advantages and disadvantages of each. I am not trying to urge particular methods on my readers.

2

The form

What to publish

Academic historians forget at their peril that family historians are by far the largest constituency among users of historical records. If we were to choose the documents for publication on the basis of meeting the greatest demand our chief criterion could only be the number of individuals they mention by name and how far what they tell us about these people is relevant to family history. Thus parish registers would emerge as a firm favourite, with probate records, hearth-tax returns, census returns all well to the fore. Census returns have mostly daunted even the most ambitious record publishers; at Portsmouth a scheme for publishing the enumerators' books for the 1851 census collapsed partly because of the sheer scale of what was needed, partly because of doubts whether there was much point in editing records so easily accessible through microfilm. But there is a distinguished history of publishing early parish registers, very notably those from London by the Register Section of the Harleian Society; the Index Library of the British Record Society has published many indexes to probate records as well as calendars of the documents themselves, and both wills and inventories have been edited for several county record societies; while quite a number of hearth-tax returns have been published already and the British Record Society is currently fostering a scheme to complete publication of at least one return – ideally one for the 1660s, one for the 1670s – for every county.

Apart from their value for family history, all these types of record are valuable for other kinds of history as well. The parish registers of Colyton in Devon were the basis for Sir Tony Wrigley's seminal work that effectively initiated the study of early-modern demography in England; Professor Margaret Spufford's work on villages in Cambridgeshire is an outstanding example of many studies of local and regional social history that have drawn important evidence from probate records; the work by Philip Styles on the hearth-tax returns of a small part of Warwickshire revealed much of the administration behind seventeenth-century taxation; and another seminal book, Professor Michael Anderson's study of Lancashire households in the nineteenth century, uses census records as its

principal source.[1] But we may doubt whether these and other comparably voluminous records are well suited for traditional publication. No more than a sample can
be offered within the scope of one or even a series of volumes; as evidence of the
nature and form of the record such a sample is unnecessary, for many have been
published already, while it goes little way to meet the needs of family historians or
others who will need to consult the full range of surviving records. Records such as
these are best made available by other means: microform, with or without indexes, is
a more practicable approach, and this is one area where electronic publication may
well resolve all the difficulties.

Many historical records are published on a one-off basis: a single work in one or
many volumes produced on the initiative of a public body or a private publisher –
thus many editions of correspondence and diaries of the past two hundred years are
commercial publications. Here, clearly, each case is decided on its merits and normally both historical value and interest to a wide readership will have played a part
in the decision to publish. But far more – and, broadly speaking, far more varied –
records are published in series, mostly by publishing societies, and here the decision
what to publish has to be taken in the context of a broader general policy. This is
more of a problem for some publishing bodies than for others. The Canterbury and
York Society, for instance, publishes little but bishops' registers from the middle
ages; all those that survive are of great historical interest and all are fully worthy of
publication. The Pipe Roll Society has diversified a little more than its name suggests, but confines itself to records of the twelfth and early thirteenth centuries; no
justification is needed to publish any surviving record of that period. At the other
end of the scale the British Academy's Records of Social and Economic History and,
even more, the Camden Series of the Royal Historical Society publish a wide variety
of records of all periods; here the publication's contribution to historical knowledge
at the national level is the normal criterion. Most publishing bodies lie between
these two extremes. Some publish records on a single topic, like the Navy Records
Society, or the Hakluyt Society, which publishes records of voyages and exploration;
here there must sometimes be difficult decisions in choosing what to publish, but
settled by criteria appropriate to the particular theme. Others publish records for a
particular area, mostly for a single historical county or, like the Surtees Society, a
more extended region; but besides Portsmouth, other cities or towns with regular

1   E.A. Wrigley, 'Family reconstitution', in *An Introduction to English Historical Demography*, ed. E.A.
     Wrigley (Cambridge Group for the History of Population and Social Structure, publication 1;
     London, 1966), pp.96–159, and E.A. Wrigley, 'Family limitation in pre-industrial England',
     Economic History Review, 2nd series 19 (1966), pp.82–109; M. Spufford, *Contrasting Communities:
     English Villages in the Sixteenth and Seventeenth Centuries* (Cambridge, 1974); introduction by P.
     Styles to *Hearth Tax Returns*, ed. M. Walker (Warwick County Records; 1957); M. Anderson, *Family
     Structure in Nineteenth Century Lancashire* (Cambridge, 1971).

series of record publications are Bristol, London, Oxford, Southampton and, impressively, Banbury.

When we look at what local record series have published we are confronted with an amazing range of material, much of it chosen with imagination and foresight. Some firm favourites appear in many of the lists. Feet of fines, cartularies, catalogues of printed county maps and archdeaconry visitation returns are among them, and a glance at each will show us something of the considerations that have to be borne in mind. Feet of fines are the records, retained by the royal courts, of fictitious suits brought to secure what amounted to the court's registration of conveyances of property; they date from the late twelfth century on, and are among the public records. They are relatively uniform in phrasing, so can be calendared with little difficulty; they are short, so a large number can be placed in a single volume which, as there is no overall pattern or structure, can be brought to a close at any point; and in the Public Record Office they are arranged county by county, so that converting them into published volumes for a county series is a fairly painless process. Cartularies, as we have already seen, are the books into which medieval estate owners copied their muniments, especially conveyances; those that survive are mostly from monasteries. What was one book in the middle ages is normally compassable within one or two printed volumes and it is a discrete, clearly demarcated source that can be seen, rightly or wrongly, as complete in itself; all this helps to commend it to both editors and publishing bodies. A complete catalogue of printed maps of a single county, from Saxton's maps of the 1570s to the late nineteenth century, a not wholly arbitrary closing date, listing successive states of the printing plates and the books in which they were published, neatly fills a single volume; that it has marketing potential to collectors and dealers in maps, as well as to the more usual public of local historians and others, gives it added appeal to a record society. Like county maps, the returns of an archdeaconry visitation fit into a single volume and, like feet of fines, they are already collected together and, uniform in layout, easily calendared – moreover, another important point for a county society, by their very nature they cover every parish, avoiding the risk that a local subscriber's home town or village never gets mentioned.

Publication of all these kinds of record – feet of fines, cartularies, county maps, visitation returns – can be fully justified on scholarly grounds: they all contribute to their own fields of historical knowledge. In showing that other considerations too may have led to their being published by local record societies I am not suggesting that it is in the least improper to take these into account. But they illustrate how the pattern of local-record publication has been unavoidably skewed in certain directions; original charters, manorial surveys, topographical prints, tithe apportionments, are of no less historical value, but have been less published simply because the dispersal of the original material, its scale and nature or its concentration on particular localities all make publication harder or less suitable. At Portsmouth – and in looking at a single place we avoid some of the difficulties of publishing for an entire county – we have maintained as our principal criterion the contribution that a particular record would make to historical knowledge, and not just at the local level: unless it was of significance in the national context it would not be worth publishing at all. We have tried to see Portsmouth's history in the context of national, even international, historical scholarship and to take into account current research and debate in deciding what to publish.

Here an important distinction must be made. In the last chapter we saw that there are serious drawbacks to letting the current agenda of historical scholarship determine how a text is edited: a better result is achieved by a wholly neutral and comprehensive approach. But this need not apply by any means to the actual choice of records to publish. On the contrary, if the volume is planned with current historical work in mind, it means not only that it will be noticed and, one would hope, be of direct value as soon as it appears, but also that its editor will be able to call on the expertise of fellow-specialists in preparing it – to its benefit. We could even say that in choosing the records to edit the best approach is the historian's, in actually editing them it is the archivist's. Certainly what is edited is one thing; how it is edited is quite another.

At Portsmouth, with what now seems amazing naivety, I proposed in 1969 a rational programme of record publication. One of our first volumes would be a definitive edition, Latin text and translation, of the successive royal charters which determined the structure of the borough's government until 1836. This would serve as a work of reference for the editor of any later volume whose documents related to the borough's officers and courts. Then, looking still to their value to future editors, there would be three bibliographies: of books and articles on Portsmouth, along with all books printed there, of maps of the area, and of pictures, whether drawings, paintings or prints. Having scholars working simultaneously on all three bibliographies would permit valuable exchange of information – maps and prints, after all, often appear in books – and we even held one useful seminar with the editors of all three to get agreement on coverage and style. We considered the possibility of further bibliographies of manuscript records and of the large-scale plans and drawings produced by architects and engineers, but postponed these to a later stage. From the start, though, we planned a subseries of volumes of the dockyard's early archives, the records that had accumulated at the dockyard itself and were now mostly at the National Maritime Museum and the Public Record Office: each volume would cover a short period and there would be an introductory volume describing the archive as a whole, perhaps with much background information in tabular form – comprehensive lists of dockyard officers, establishment and other costs over the years, lists of ships built and so on.

The editor

General editors and editorial boards may propose, but it is the editor of the individual volume who disposes, every time. In saying this I emphatically and sincerely do not intend the faintest hint of reproach towards the editor of any volume I have ever been responsible for: without exception they have been conscientious, careful and thoroughly co-operative. Unforeseen career changes can make it wholly impossible for an editor to meet what originally seemed a realistic schedule. Distance can produce problems all its own – one of our Portsmouth editors moved to Peru, another to the North-West Territories of Canada (the polar bear on his letterhead was something of a consolation). And, even without dramatic developments of this kind, it can be impossibly difficult for the editor of historical records to estimate at all accurately how long the work will take. Unpredictable difficulties abound: new records come to light, distant sources have to be checked, it is impossible to work from microfilm as expected because the original manuscripts are too faint or too badly damaged or too tightly bound, to everyone's surprise the apparently straightforward text throws up a mass of complex queries – and so on. Anyone who has ever edited a text will sympathise with these and the many other difficulties that arise. There is no cure for them and no way of guarding against them in advance. And, what every record series council or editorial board learns to recognise, no sanction whatever is available to induce an editor to complete the task – nor, indeed, could this be desirable: rushed work is the very last thing one would wish in an edited text.

Unavoidable delays of one kind or another have meant that the Portsmouth Record Series as published is quite different from the rational sequence of volumes that was planned. Professor Geoffrey Martin's magnificent edition of the royal charters has appeared, but as the ninth volume, not the second; of the projected bibliographies, the only one so far published is Mr Donald Hodson's catalogue of Portsmouth maps before 1801, a most important work in the history of cartography; but the bibliography of books is now nearly ready as a part of a county-wide bibliography for the whole of Hampshire, having moved outside the confines of the Portsmouth series. At an early stage, when I began to realise that a planned publication programme was not going to work, I asked Mr William Kellaway, then general editor of the London Record Society, which was producing an annual volume with clockwork regularity, for the secret of his success. His answer was memorable: he always knew what volume would next go to press, but as to what would follow it a year later he could as soon spot the next Derby winner. Even if one keeps in close touch with one's editors – and this, surely, must be a *sine qua non* – and even in the final stages of the work, unexpected delays often make it impossible to predict its completion date. A comforting corollary for a general editor is that whereas it often seems as if in eighteen months' time, to one's utter embarrassment, some six or seven completed texts are going to arrive simultaneously on one's desk, in point of fact this never actually happens.

I have been writing as though finding an editor was the least of the problems in commissioning a projected edition. It is anything but. One is, after all, asking a specialist to devote – if the work is done as it should be – a significant portion of a life's scholarly output to a project of someone else's devising, a project, moreover, that, as we have seen, is likely to bring less kudos, do less to advance an academic career, than the same amount of work expended on writing a monograph. This, of course, is overstating the case. The project may have been devised by the publishing body or its general editor, but for its detailed form and contents they are bound to rely heavily on the knowledge and advice of the specialist editor, and its eventual shape will be, at the very least, the outcome of collaboration. Again, the specialist who undertakes the work will have full knowledge of the relevant background, historical and archival, and may well have already done much of the necessary transcription. A monograph and an edition of a principal source produced together will demand significantly less time and effort than the two works produced independently by different scholars. Moreover, the certainty of publication is attractive, especially if, as at Portsmouth, the publishing body produces high-quality books to professional standards. The publishing body need not feel it has nothing to offer.

At the same time it can be extremely difficult to find editors even for projects that are widely accepted as thoroughly worthwhile. An example is the work on the plans and drawings of architects and engineers that the Portsmouth series envisaged from the start, a project which would complement the catalogues of maps and pictures, would break new and very interesting ground in the national context, and would almost certainly lead to historical discoveries of some importance. But the few established scholars with relevant expertise are fully committed elsewhere and, lying outside the more usual fields of history and art history, it is unlikely to attract those at the start of their careers. It is a depressing fact that the more innovative, the more original, a project is, the harder it is to find anyone to work on it.

Luckily, however, it is not only the publishing body and its general editor who have to initiate record publications. I soon learned that in practice one comes to rely heavily on chance offers: casual conversations that reveal work in an unusual or interesting field that could lead to record publication, documents worked on for a thesis or book that could be used as a basis for an edition, and so on. Several notable volumes in the Portsmouth Record Series came this way, among them Edwin Welch's calendar of records of adult education, 1886–1939, which opened up an interesting and important field of social history, and Mr J.A. Lowe's edition of Marine Corps records, 1764–1800, which filled an extraordinary gap in scholarly work on the eighteenth-century armed forces. Flexibility rather than planned strategy is in fact the only practicable policy, learning to be willing and ready to draw imaginatively on whatever talent or expertise is available.

Strategy of choice

One way or another, then, publishers of historical records have less unfettered choice in what they publish than may appear. But some choice they certainly have, and they at once come up against one question that we found ourselves confronting at Portsmouth. Thinking of historians – of every kind – working in Portsmouth, we could see the need to make available to them sources for Portsmouth's history in distant repositories. Conversely we could see it as our task to make widely available the historical sources preserved in Portsmouth. It is not just a question for local record series: does the Camden Series, say, have a duty to give the world the historical sources that are available in Britain, or rather to bring to British scholars sources for British history that exist abroad? The answer in most cases will, of course, be both, though a record publishing body may choose to lay particular stress on one or the other. At Portsmouth, certainly, we have acknowledged an obligation in both directions, seeing ourselves as performing a service both in making adult-education records in Cambridge University's archives available to Portsmouth local historians and in publishing the surviving divisional records of the Marine Corps from the City Records Office and the Royal Marines Museum at Portsmouth. In both cases we adhered strictly to our rule that the records we publish should be of interest and value in the national historical context.

One sort of publication that has special value brings together records of a single type that are scattered in different repositories. The Portsmouth catalogue of maps comes in this category as well as the other planned bibliographies. So too does Mrs K.A. Hanna's edition of all surviving private charters or deeds from the Portsmouth area down to 1547: nearly 1200 documents, which she discovered in repositories that include Northumberland Record Office, Nottingham University Library, the *archives départementales* of Seine-Maritime and the municipal library at Avranches. A volume in preparation by Dr David Postles will print all surviving records of medieval estate administration from the area; they are less far-flung than the charters, but will all the same serve the same valuable purpose in permitting comparison and cross-reference between closely related records that an individual searcher can bring together only with difficulty.

But in planning volumes of this kind we have insisted on two conditions. One is that what is brought together should be defined in archival, not thematic, terms. They should all be one kind of document, not a variety of records dealing with a common subject. The reason is bound up with the advantages we have seen in publishing records in such a way that they will be of use to any future enquiry, foreseen or unforeseen. To produce a volume of varied records on, say, crime in eighteenth-century Portsmouth may produce a work of great value to anyone working on eighteenth-century crime – but of limited value to anyone else, such as the student of, say, the victualling trade, whose need will be met patchily and by good luck if at all. Far better to publish the borough sessions papers as a class (whether preserved together or dispersed), thus dealing evenhandedly with every relevant topic and giving every enquirer the assurance of full coverage of this particular source. Our second condition for a volume bringing together collected material is that it should be comprehensive within clearly defined limits, so that the reader can be sure everything discoverable is included. These two conditions are closely linked, and they lead straight into the thorny question of volumes of select documents.

Selections of documents

At first sight there is no problem here. If we accept that edited records should be presented objectively, with no preconceptions about the use that is to be made of them, there can be no place for select texts, for selection on any but a random basis at once introduces a subjective, value-laden or even personal element. In any case, as Dr Hunnisett points out, 'No selective publication of records can be an adequate substitute for a comprehensive edition'.[2] I am in entire agreement. Certainly there is a long and distinguished tradition of publishing select texts, and one thinks particularly of the Selden Society, which for over a hundred years has produced editions of select legal cases, chosen from records far too voluminous for any sort of comprehensive publication to be practicable. But this only underlines the point. The Society's publications admirably illustrate the development of particular aspects of law, the workings of particular courts, and pinpoint key cases which can be seen to demonstrate some accepted or evolving principle. They give the legal historian what is needed – but only the legal historian: the social historian, the economic historian, to whom these records may be no less valuable, can make only limited use of these texts. Moreover the legal historian has to accept the subjective judgment of the editor as to which cases are interesting or significant, which are not. To test this judgment, to seek further evidence, needs recourse to the original records – to which, of course, the published select cases will have provided an admirable introduction: the searcher will be able to find the way round these records, their layout, their structure, their technicalities of procedure and vocabulary. Such an edition can be very valuable – but we must accept its inevitable limitations.

The first book I ever reviewed points to further limitations – dangers, even – of editions of select documents. This was the edition by Madeleine Elsass of letters of

2   *Editing Records for Publication* (BRA, Archives and the User, no.4; 1977), p.13.

1782–1860 from the records of the Dowlais Iron Company – a fascinating collection chosen from a large archive and arranged under broad subject headings: 'Markets and sales', 'Technical', and so on.[3] But in the words of my review,

> The letters printed have necessarily been selected as of particular interest rather than as a typical sample of the correspondence: thus there are a number of letters of complaint about the quality of the firm's products, but hardly any from the satisfied customers who must always have been in the majority.[4]

After all, letters ordering iron rails, saying they have arrived and are just what was wanted and then sending payment do not easily make gripping reading.

In fact, what is one to do, confronted, as Madeleine Elsass was, with an archive that includes 563,000 original letters? It would be defeatist to say that there is no way they can properly be published. The select edition gives a view – even if too highly coloured – of the nature and style of the correspondence: it whets the appetite admirably. Quoting again my review,

> Few of the letters [published] form consecutive series, and one is often left tantalizingly in the dark about the outcome of the matters mentioned. This is both the book's strength and its weakness. One suspects that it will bring many more historians – both professional and amateur – into the County Record Office to work on the original papers than any formal catalogue could do.[5]

What such an edition cannot do, except in very limited cases, is serve as a substitute for work on the records themselves; it cannot fulfil the same scholarly purpose as the edition of a single record, or a discrete group, though there is the risk that some may suppose that it can. It offers instead a first introduction, a way in to records whose sheer bulk makes comprehensive publication impossible, but which can be explored further through photocopies or microfilms or at the record office.

Though it is most obviously records of the past 300 years that pose this problem of sheer bulk, earlier records are not immune from it. The plea rolls of the court of King's Bench from the thirteenth century onwards, one of the series from which the Selden Society has published select cases, is an archive of the same order of magnitude as the half-million letters of the Dowlais Iron Company. Even in publishing the manorial accounts for Cuxham from 1276 to 1359 selection was necessary: to print all those surviving would have called for two 800-page volumes, not one, and besides all the earliest and all the latest I published a random sample of the rest, two small

3   *Iron in the Making: Dowlais Iron Company Letters 1782–1860*, ed. M. Elsass (Glamorgan Quarter Sessions and County Council, and Guest Keen Iron and Steel Co. Ltd, 1960).

4   *Journal of the Society of Archivists*, 2 (1960–4), p.82.

5   *ibid.*, pp.82–3.

groups of consecutive accounts – consecutive to provide a broader picture, showing how cash, corn and livestock were carried over from one year to the next.

Sometimes the question arises of publishing a record that is itself a selection of documents, usually copies. The selection itself may be of archival and historical significance. Virtually all medieval cartularies are in this category: copies of those documents deemed worthy of permanent record from the archives of the monastery or other landowner. Besides the actual texts of the documents, which ones were chosen and how they were arranged can be of interest to the historian, and there can be no difficulty in justifying publication of the cartulary as it stands. However, a problem arises when original documents survive that have been entered in the cartulary – or others from the same archive that have been left out. Clearly the text of the original is to be preferred to the cartulary copy and should replace it in the printed edition – with notes of the copy's variants – even if the cartulary's ordering of the documents is retained. If only a few documents left out of the cartulary survive from the archive they may conveniently be placed in an appendix, as in Audrey Woodcock's edition of the cartulary of St Gregory's Priory, Canterbury.[6] If there are more, they may be interspersed among the cartulary copies, as in the monumental edition of the Lincoln *Registrum Antiquissimum* by C.W. Foster and Kathleen Major[7] – though this may run the risk of obscuring the contents of the cartulary, while presenting the documents in an arrangement less than ideal for the modern searcher. It is arguably better, if there are many additional documents, to abandon the arrangement of the cartulary altogether, while recording its make-up, and to use it simply as one source for the collection of documents ordered entirely by the editor; this was the way H.E. Salter published well over 900 deeds of medieval Oxford that had come from the archives of St John Baptist Hospital there – only 171 had been included in the hospital's thirteenth-century cartulary.[8]

Cartularies are an outstanding case of selections of documents made for a functional purpose. There are others, such as the collections of precedents made by lawyers, medieval and modern or – an interesting case of historical records printed for a practical purpose – the volume of relevant extracts from manorial court rolls of 1462–1864 that a local committee for the preservation of Wimbledon Common in Surrey published in 1866.[9] There is a fundamental distinction between these and the collections of copied documents made, not for functional use but for general

---

6   *Cartulary of the Priory of St. Gregory, Canterbury*, ed. A.M. Woodcock (Camden 3rd Series, 88; 1956).

7   *The Registrum Antiquissimum of the Cathedral Church of Lincoln*, ed. C.W. Foster and K. Major (Lincoln Record Society; 10v. and facsimiles, 1931–73).

8   *A Cartulary of the Hospital of St. John the Baptist*, ed. H.E. Salter (Oxford Historical Society; 3v., 1914–17).

9   *Extracts from the Court Rolls of the Manor of Wimbledon*, [ed. P.H. Lawrence] (London, 1866).

interest, by historians and antiquaries – what we might call select texts in manuscript, suffering from the same drawbacks as select texts in print. Sometimes, however, the collection contains copies of documents that have since been lost. The
volume of copies of medieval documents made in about 1640–1 and known as Sir
Christopher Hatton's book of seals is a case in point: some of the important early
charters it records are now lost, and from others the seals have disappeared, among
them the seal of William the Conqueror's half-brother, Bishop Odo of Bayeux, now
known only from the apparently careful drawing in this volume.[10] An example of a
similar collection of more modern records is the volume of transcripts and summaries of what had been judged particularly interesting letters from letter-books of
1711–1813 in the Customs house at Liverpool, correspondence between the local
Customs officials and the Board of Customs in London. The original letter-books
were destroyed in a Second World War air-raid, so that the copied selection is now
all we know of their contents.[11] Both these collections, the book of seals and the letter-book extracts, have been published, justifiably – though, looking at the national
rather than the local picture, it seems a little perverse to have published the
Liverpool extracts when complete series of Customs letter-books survive from so
many other ports. Clearly every case like these must be decided on its merits,
though one must be wary of the temptation to accept the selection of texts made by
someone in the past simply because it is so much easier than making a principled
selection oneself.

At Portsmouth we first met the problem of selection in the dockyard papers, the
records that had accumulated in the dockyard itself, crucially important to the history of Portsmouth and of the Royal Navy. The surviving archive from the late seventeenth century to the late nineteenth, now in the National Maritime Museum and
the Public Record Office, is of broadly the same order of magnitude as the medieval
plea rolls or the correspondence of the Dowlais Iron Company. We planned a series
of volumes, each for some ten to fifteen years, which sooner or later will cover much
of the eighteenth and nineteenth centuries: the volume for 1774–83, edited by Dr
R.J.B. Knight, has already been published,[12] those for 1749–63 (Mr G.G. Harris) and
1852–69 (Dr C.I. Hamilton) are far advanced. But even for these short periods nothing like complete publication is possible: from 1774–83 there survive twenty-five volumes of correspondence in and out, nearly all of it between the dockyard officers and
the Navy Board in London, some 6000 pages of copied letters, orders, returns and
reports. Our aim was to make available as much as possible of this mass of material

---

10   *Sir Christopher Hatton's Book of Seals*, ed. L.C. Loyd and D.M. Stenton (Oxford, 1950), plate VIII.
11   *Customs Letter-Books of the Port of Liverpool 1711–1813*, ed. R.C. Jarvis (Chetham Society, 3rd series 6;
      1954); the editor comments candidly on the drawbacks of such a selection (p.v).
12   PthRS, 6.

in a form that could be of direct value to the researcher, while serving as a guide to what had had to be left unpublished.

After careful consideration and much discussion with Dr Knight, whose volume was to set the pattern for all the dockyard paper volumes, what we settled on was an adapted version of the system used by Madeleine Elsass for the Dowlais Iron Company's letters. We began, however, with an innovation: all the correspondence from a sample week edited in full, sixty-four items which took thirty pages of print. This serves to show the detailed character of the correspondence and to introduce specimens of regular daily and weekly reports. For the rest the volume is divided into nine thematic sections: Buildings and docks, Incidents and accidents, Stores and contracts, and so on. Within each section a selection of letters is calendared, not edited in full, but with many direct quotations, grouping together those concerning a particular operation or incident; where only a part of a sequence of letters is calendared, references are given to other relevant items with the gist of their contents, so that events are not left hanging in mid-air. The letters calendared are concerned not only with outstanding events, such as the destruction of the rope-house by arson in 1776 and the sinking of the *Royal George* in 1782, but also with as full a range as possible of typical and routine operations; two often recurring matters, the disciplining of dockyard workers and large contracts with suppliers, are entered in the form of annual lists. Appendices include the full texts of some forms of document that do not occur in the fully edited sample week, calendared specimens of regular orders, reports or returns that were sent every year, every quarter, every month or on occasion, and tables of information drawn from the papers as a whole, among them impressive lists showing what ship occupied each of the six docks, and why, every day of the ten-year period.

If the bulk of the records dictates selection in publication, this seems a way of achieving it that avoids many pitfalls; the sample week, the references to continuations of correspondence, the specimen texts and tables all remove potential shortcomings. Although the division of the documents into thematic sections recalls the drawbacks of a volume of thematically selected records, these drawbacks are much diminished when we are dealing with a relatively small tranche of a single archive. We are in no doubt that the 1774–83 volume is a satisfactory model for the dockyard papers of other periods.

However, for the eighteenth-century letter-books of the Customs house at Portsmouth we decided on a different strategy.[13] These had had better luck in the Second World War than the corresponding records at Liverpool: the books with copies of in-letters survive from 1726 on, and of out-letters for 1748–50 and then from 1760. No Customs records of this kind had been published apart from the

13   PthRS, 8.

selection from Liverpool and as, besides their local interest, they throw interesting light on the Customs administration in general there seemed good reason to devote a volume to those from Portsmouth. Our aim here was to open up all Customs records relating to Portsmouth from the re-organisation of 1671 to the mid-eighteenth century, while producing a volume that would serve also as a starting-point for work on the later records in these series or on the corresponding records from other ports – and also as an introduction to relevant records from the central Board of Customs in London. The edition, by Mr G. Hampson, prints the whole of the first out-letter book, September 1748 to September 1750, and the in-letter books covering the same period as well as the previous eight months, from January 1748, to show the pattern when we have only one side of the correspondence. The letters are printed in full, but with address, salutation and valediction summarised. The introduction gives an historical account of the Customs organisation and its work from 1671 to the time of the published letters, and describes the surviving central records for the same period. Among the appendices are the Portsmouth entries in the central register of seized contraband and tables of Customs employees and salaries at Portsmouth from 1671 to 1750.

This strategy has many advantages. Admittedly it makes directly available only a tiny portion of the archive and does not cover important occurrences at other points in the period – but they can be brought out, with relevant references, in the introduction, and the text printed has the enormous merits of being complete, typical and incontrovertibly objective. To this extent it gives a more precise picture of the archive – and thus opens it up no less effectively – than the thematic calendar and summaries that seek to present a larger portion. Moreover, any searcher can use what is there for any purpose without having to wonder whether the selection process, however careful and objective, may not have distorted the picture for the particular enquiry. But despite these advantages, I do not think we made a wrong decision in choosing the alternative strategy for the dockyard papers – they are simply two different solutions to the problem. The variety of the dockyard papers and the significance of the events they record would make publication of a typical tranche for each ten to fifteen year period less appropriate – it would not do them full justice. But for the more homogeneous work of the Customs at Portsmouth this approach works well, and we are using it again for Mr Matthew Sheldon's edition of the records from the Victualling Board's Portsmouth office, publishing two of the earliest surviving letter-books, which begin in 1756.

From catalogue to full edition

By now it may well be thought that some explanation is called for. We are considering the editing of historical documents; but I have been writing not only of full editions of texts, but also of calendars, summaries, and even catalogues, bibliographies and indexes. Have I not been straying from my theme? Let us have another look at our two spectra, the historian's and the archivist's, which both have the edited text at one end. We have seen that if we move even a little way along the historian's spectrum, from the full edition to select documents, we begin to sacrifice the neutrality that I see as the *raison d'être* of editing texts – and the further we move along this spectrum, to the volume of *pièces justificatives*, to the appendix of documents, to the footnote quotations, we move more and more to work where the document is there in a supporting role, subordinate to the historical argument: no matter how closely based on the documents, it is historical interpretation that sets the agenda, not the documents themselves. Some record-publishing bodies see nothing anomalous in moving along the whole length of this spectrum; they see the monograph and the edition simply as different ways of presenting the past, which speaks either with its own voice or through the voice of the historian. The Chetham Society in particular has published not only many records of Lancashire and Cheshire but also many valuable studies of the region's history – in my own field, medieval economic history, G.H. Tupling's book on the economic history of Rossendale and Dr P.H.W. Booth's study of medieval administration in Cheshire come at once to mind as works of outstanding importance.[14] Certainly there is the need in every part of the country for an outlet for publishing just such scholarly works of local and regional history; I should be the last to suggest that there is anything wrong with publishing historical monographs and, after all, to assist the publication of interpretative studies is a prime reason for publishing records in the first place. On the other hand, to mingle monographs and editions in this way to my mind is to muddy the waters badly, running the risk of confusing authentic record and historical interpretation. Far better to make a clear distinction between the two – as the Royal Historical Society does, keeping its series of Studies in History quite separate from the edited texts of the Camden Series.

If, on the other hand, we move along our other spectrum, the archivist's, we do not meet the same drawbacks. Our first stage from the edited text is the calendar, a word familiar to medieval and early-modern historians, unknown, I have found, to many late-modernists, which means simply a précis of the text, omitting common form and other verbiage. We move then successively to the summary, the short catalogue description or the entries of an index. Each stage tells us less and less about the document, to be sure, but at each stage the document itself sets the agenda, is what the whole operation is about, and there is no reason why a catalogue or an index

---

14   G.H. Tupling, *The Economic History of Rossendale* (Chetham Society, new series 86; 1927); P.H.W. Booth, *The Financial Administration of the Lordship and County of Chester, 1272–1377* (Chetham Society, 3rd series 28; 1981).

should be any less neutral in its presentation than a fully edited text. The reader may at once question this. Is not calendaring a document a form of thematic selection? – internal selection of part of its contents, rather than external selection of documents from a group. We shall look later at the process of calendaring and the many possible pitfalls, but the answer must be that a neutral all-purpose presentation is the unquestioned objective at every point along the archivist's spectrum. Publication in any of these forms is publication of records, in a way that publication of a mono-graph, however important in its interpretation of these records, however closely based on them, simply is not.

It was this line of reasoning that led the board at Portsmouth to accept the idea of publication at any point along this archivist's spectrum – whichever point seemed appropriate in the particular case. And given the new ease of access to so many records, given the advent of cheap photocopying, it seemed sensible to move further along the spectrum, away from the full edition, than could have been justified earlier. The policy adopted is printed in every volume:

> It is proposed to print complete texts only of three types of record: first, a very few doc-uments that are of basic importance to the history of the City; second, any records of Portsmouth that are sufficiently unusual to give their publication more than purely local interest; and third, records of types found elsewhere but hitherto unpublished. For the rest the Series will consist of calendars, catalogues, indexes and bibliographies.

Within these guidelines there is room for quite wide choice; often, as we have seen in looking at the dockyard papers and the Customs letter-books, one has to decide whether to publish a little about a large number of records or a lot – even full tran-scripts – about a few. Each case must be decided on its merits – there can be no rule of thumb.

The electronic edition

Now, of course, there is a new question to be asked: is traditional publication appro-priate for the particular record, or are there such enormous advantages in electronic publication that there is little point in embarking on a printed volume? We can no longer view electronic media as too ephemeral, too light-weight, to be entrusted with learned work; no one now doubts that scholarship can be presented as well on screen as in print, that scholarly standards are no less secure and that in this form it need be no less permanent, even if we may still reasonably ask just how this perma-nence will be ultimately achieved. Already we can see how much easier it is to consult work available on the Internet – all that is needed is a screen with appropriate access – than if it is in a book that has to be owned or borrowed or visited in a library.

The advantages of electronic publication are so obvious that they hardly need to be rehearsed. That the length or scale of publication is no longer constrained by the limits of printed volumes, that the material can be arranged in more than one order, that passages from different parts can be placed side by side, that it can be searched automatically and in a highly sophisticated way for particular words or combinations of letters – all these are enormous gains. Efficient searching is possible only on a fully normalised text, but this normalised version need not obtrude itself on the reader if it is not wanted for any other purpose; it may seem tidier to keep it behind the scenes. In any case it is harder to get away with inconsistencies on the screen than in print. One potential advantage was demonstrated at an early stage by Dr C.M. Woolgar in his work on the Wellington papers at Southampton University Library: starting with a simple catalogue of the archive, entries can be upgraded to points further along the archivist's spectrum, as time, opportunity or funding allows, so that what began as a catalogue can be transformed by gradual stages into a full edition.[15] Certainly, as I said in the first chapter, though before long we may well find that traditional printed editions are in decline, it will probably be a considerable time before this form of publication is entirely superseded. All the same, for certain kinds of record electronic publication already offers so very much more, that a publishing body ought now to commit itself to print only after careful reflection.

An outstanding example is medieval private charters or deeds. By far the most numerous type of record to survive from the middle ages, we certainly have still a great deal to learn from them. As we have seen, they have been published mostly as collections of documents accumulated by a single landowner, a single recipient, especially from the copies brought together in a cartulary. However, there have been a few editions, all of them important, of the collected early charters not received but issued by a single magnate family, such as those of the Mowbrays by Professor D.E. Greenway, or of the Redvers by Dr Robert Bearman.[16] Fewer still are editions of deeds, of any owner or any grantor, that relate to a single part of the country; Sir Frank Stenton's edition of early charters from the Danelaw is a notable example, and another is the ten volumes of Yorkshire deeds edited by William Brown and others,[17] while at Portsmouth we are about to break new ground by publishing, what these collections are not, a comprehensive edition by Mrs K.A. Hanna of all surviving

15   C.M. Woolgar, 'The Wellington papers database: an interim report', *Journal of the Society of Archivists*, 9 (1988), pp.1–20.

16   *Charters of the Honour of Mowbray 1107–1191*, ed. D.E. Greenway (Brit.Ac., RSEH, new series 1; 1972); *Charters of the Redvers Family and the Earldom of Devon, 1090–1217*, ed. R. Bearman (Devon and Cornwall Record Society, new series 37; 1994).

17   *Documents Illustrative of the Social and Economic History of the Danelaw from Various Collections*, ed. F.M. Stenton (Brit.Ac., RSEH, old series 5; 1920); *Yorkshire Deeds*, ed. W. Brown et al. (Yorkshire Archaeological Society, Record Series; 10v., 1909–55).

private deeds relating to the area before the end of Henry VIII's reign.[18] Each of these methods of publishing these deeds – by recipient, by grantor, by area – offers its own insights, opening the way to revealing comparisons when the documents are placed side by side. Before starting work on the volume of Portsmouth area deeds, Mrs Hanna produced an important edition of the three cartularies of Southwick Priory, published in the Hampshire Record Series; many of the Portsmouth deeds are in these cartularies and these, for the sake of completeness, have had to be printed a second time in the Portsmouth volume, though in severely summarised form. The two projects were planned together in 1978–9; if initiated now, what emerged would surely be a single electronic edition of all the documents, which at the click of a key could be assembled by grantor, by recipient, by place or in any other way. Medieval deeds are not the only kind of record peculiarly suited to treatment in electronic form: similar arguments could be applied to catalogues or collected reproductions of topographical prints, drawings and paintings. For all these the advantages of electronic publication must now be very seriously considered before embarking on a traditional printed edition.

So far, more work has been done on electronic editions of literary texts than of records. However, in Sheffield University's Humanities Research Institute the fifteen electronic editing projects now under way include not only monumental editions of all manuscripts of the Canterbury Tales and of all early editions of John Foxe's *Book of Martyrs* but also publication of the first Earl of Strafford's papers and of other groups of records.[19] Again, Cambridge University Press is about to publish an edition on compact disk of the fourteenth- and fifteenth-century rolls of the English parliament – the *Rotuli Parliamentorum* – giving full original text and translation. At the other end of the archivist's spectrum much work is in progress to give Internet access to record offices' catalogues and other finding aids. The Public Record Office's catalogues became available in 1999, and already this has produced some re-thinking for a Portsmouth Record Series volume: the global search facility led to the unexpected discovery – pleasing but disconcerting – of a whole cache of eighteenth-century Portsmouth victualling-yard letter-books lurking among the records from Plymouth dockyard, volumes in the same sequence as those that Mr Matthew Sheldon is editing for the series.[20] Projects to bring all record offices' catalogues on to the Internet, begun in Scotland (Scottish Archives Network), are now being planned in both England (Access to Archives) and Wales (Archives Network Wales). We may see electronic calendars and edited texts developed by upgrading these finding aids, as demonstrated by Dr Woolgar from the Wellington papers. More

18   PthRS, 11.
19   Details of these and other projects are on the Institute's website <http://www.shef.ac.uk/uni/academic/D-H/hri>.
20   PRO, ADM 174/294–298.

likely, though, as the remaining difficulties are smoothed out and as the new technology becomes ever more familiar, its advantages ever more obvious, we shall simply see more and more record-publishing bodies turning to publication in electronic form.

The translated edition

Whether publication is electronic or printed, another question to be decided by anyone producing a full edition of most medieval and many early-modern records is that of translation. The records are in Latin or, very occasionally, French. The days are long past when any gentleman or lady might reasonably be supposed to have a good working knowledge of Latin,[21] and although one might properly look for this – one does not always find it – in specialists whose work is based on Latin documents, one might hope that a published record would be of more general interest and value. And it is the specialists, after all, who are best placed to consult the original document, photocopy or microfilm. As one distinguished medieval economic historian put it, discussing how the Winchester pipe rolls – the medieval bishops' estate accounts – were to be published, 'Translation will reach the widest possible public – the specialists can look after themselves'.

Medieval estate accounts are notoriously difficult records to use: they abound in various kinds of fictitious entries, and to believe literally what they tell us could give rise to strange misconceptions. In this same discussion I was amused to catch myself thinking that it might be too risky to make them easily accessible to local historians and others who would probably misunderstand them – just the same argument as was used for centuries, perhaps more reasonably, against translating the Bible into modern languages. But the answer, of course, is not to hide the record from the wider public by publishing in Latin, but to encourage the wider public to acquire the background knowledge needed to read the record with proper understanding. Medieval estate accounts merely present in an acute form the problem that arises with any record source, Latin or English: it was not written to inform us about the age that produced it, but to serve some wholly practical purpose at the time. If we try to use it without fully understanding what that purpose was, if we treat archival sources as a straightforward information retrieval service, we shall find they tell us things that never happened and fail to tell us what really did. With this word of caution – which we shall return to – there seems every reason to make the record as widely available as possible, to specialist and layman alike, translating it if it was not written in English.

21 '... one must not be severe on a lady's Latin', wrote John Horace Round in 1899, noting that Kate Norgate had unfortunately read 'quingentas marcas' as 5000 marks (J.H. Round, *The Commune of London* (Westminster, 1899), p.113). Can male chauvinism go further?

But, to be fair, a specialist does have particular needs that a printed edition might reasonably be expected to meet, and one of these is to know precisely what words were used, what technical turns of phrase, in the original Latin document. They are often of great significance, and are anyway what one has to work with in the manuscript records. For the specialist the fully translated document can be no more than a guide to the contents of the record, to be used as a calendared version rather than as an edited text. However, just as a calendar can be of great value to anyone, specialists included, as a guide to the record, so too can a translation. After many years' work on medieval manorial accounts I can read one of these documents as easily as I can read the daily paper, but confronted with a royal court's record of a contemporary lawsuit on closely related matters I am – let me be honest – very glad of a translation to lead me through the complexities of form and phrasing, though equally I should want to know what the original actually said.

One answer to this is to do as the Selden Society does, and provide parallel text and translation; but this instantly halves the amount that can be published and is probably best confined to important short texts. At Portsmouth Professor Martin edited the city's royal charters with text and a distinguished translation side by side, while Mrs Hanna in her calendar of private deeds provides also the full Latin texts down to 1230; it is just at this point that regular formulas replace the idiosyncrasies of earlier phrasing, but recent work on the dating of undated deeds suggests that even in these formulas nuances of wording and word order may have a significance hitherto overlooked. A more generally practicable answer is the solution eventually adopted by the Hampshire Record Series for the Winchester pipe rolls: only a full translation is printed, but microfiches of the original record are supplied in a pocket at the end of the book.[22] This has the great advantage that the specialist can refer not just to the Latin of the original, but to its layout, its handwriting, the actual letter-forms of doubtful readings; the disadvantage, however, is that the home of even the most dedicated specialist may well not contain a microfiche reader. Certainly if a text is published in full translation it should follow the pattern of Dr Mark Page's editions of these records: they are rigorously consistent, so that any Latin word in the particular document is rendered always by the same English equivalent – especially important when dealing with the words used, for example, for livestock of different ages, for different varieties of corn, for farm implements and their parts. The Latin originals of some 300 of these equivalents are then listed in a glossary.

There should be no conflict between what the specialist and the non-specialist look for in edited records. An editor sensitive to the needs of any potential reader of the text should be able to accommodate them all. The interest, the value, of the edition lies in the text itself – and that is open to anyone who cares to read it.

22   *The Pipe Roll of the Bishopric of Winchester 1301–2*, and *The Pipe Roll of the Bishopric of Winchester 1409–10*, both ed. M. Page (Hampshire Record Series, 14, 16; 1996, 1999).

3

The text

The quest for accuracy

It is time to look at the first of the three rules that must be observed in editing record texts – the only three rules, remember: in the last resort nothing else really matters. The first rule is even more important than the other two. It can be stated in two words:

Be accurate.

The reader may think this too obvious to be worth saying at all. It is not. One does not have to look far to find mistakes in published record texts; lack of expertise and sheer carelessness play their part in this, but, as we shall see, great care is needed to avoid simple error and even great care is not always successful. Yet it is not just that an inaccurate text totally fails to achieve its purpose; it negates the whole point of an edition and does positive harm.

When teaching palaeography I used to start the first session by asking everyone to copy exactly a short passage from the edited text of a sixteenth-century will, written in English – a passage of, to modern eyes, moderate but not extreme oddity of spelling and punctuation. It never failed to bring home the difficulty of copying accurately, even without any palaeographical difficulties. To a few, very few, it comes naturally; the rest of us have to try to learn the art. Roger Ellis tells how new recruits to the Public Record Office were introduced to it in the 1930s:

> The quest for accuracy ... was genuine and universal. To the young entrant, the making of office copies was the introduction to this exacting discipline: the heading to be written out precisely in the prescribed form, the text to be transcribed and extended (and that meant, to be understood) without fault or blemish; one error the hawk-eyed examiner would allow, and himself correct; one more – and back came the folio to be copied again.[1]

In the Department of Manuscripts at the British Museum, when I joined the staff in

---

1   R.H. Ellis, 'The British archivist and his Society', *Journal of the Society of Archivists*, 3 (1965–9), p.4

the 1950s, the equivalent exercise was to calendar a hundred medieval deeds from the Additional Charters, writing out the calendar entry by hand on a blue slip; they had to be written and rewritten until they were correct. 'I've had people on the verge of tears,' my novice-master remarked cheerfully, 'when they've been told to copy out their charter slips for the fourth or fifth time'. These procedures may or may not have succeeded in instilling accuracy; they certainly instilled a clear understanding of how difficult it is to achieve.

The moral for the editor of record texts is to check the final text carefully with the original documents – and then check again. One useful safeguard is always to check proofs of the text against the manuscripts themselves, not against the editor's transcription. And the moral for the general editor of a series is always to check the entire text, or at very least a substantial sample, against the actual records – never mind that it is a long, slow job, or that the text is the work of a meticulously careful editor: Homer nods, and a second eye will always spot mistakes that the first eye has missed. Ensuring accuracy is what general editors are for.

It is enormously important. A mistake in a monograph or other secondary work is bad enough: it can mislead, distort our understanding, mark a retreat of the frontiers of knowledge. But a mistake in an edited text is far worse: it amounts to falsification of what other scholars will regard as primary evidence, a virus that spreads errors in often unexpected directions over a long period. When I first worked on the medieval records of Cuxham in Oxfordshire I came across a peasant family called in the records Turnestone (with variants) – each *n* written as two minim strokes and thus, as normal in hands of the period, indistinguishable from *u* (fig.1). Turnstone seemed at least a plausible topographical surname, and this is what I called the family in my thesis and in the book based on it. Before I published my edition of the Cuxham records I luckily discovered that there is a place in Buckinghamshire called Turweston – from which my peasant family took their name, really written Turuestone.[2] There is a significant risk that future dictionaries of medieval surnames will include Turnstone as a rare Oxfordshire name; the risk would have become an irrecoverable certainty if the error had persisted in the edited texts. Some of Lucy Toulmin Smith's mistaken readings in her edition of the York cycle of mystery plays were included in her glossary as previously unrecorded words; from this they passed into the *Oxford English Dictionary*, then, much later, into the *Middle English Dictionary* – and are now all but unstoppable.[3] The trouble is that errors of

2   P.D.A. Harvey, *A Medieval Oxfordshire Village: Cuxham 1240–1400* (London, 1965), Turnstone; *Man.Rec.Cux.*, Turweston.

3   A. Brown, 'The text, the bibliographer, and the librarian', in *Otium et negotium: Studies in Onomatology and Library Science Presented to Olof von Feilitzen*, ed. F. Sandgren (Acta Bibliothecae Regiae Stockholmiensis, 16; 1973), p.25. Tantalisingly, the words thus contributed to the medieval English vocabulary are not there identified.

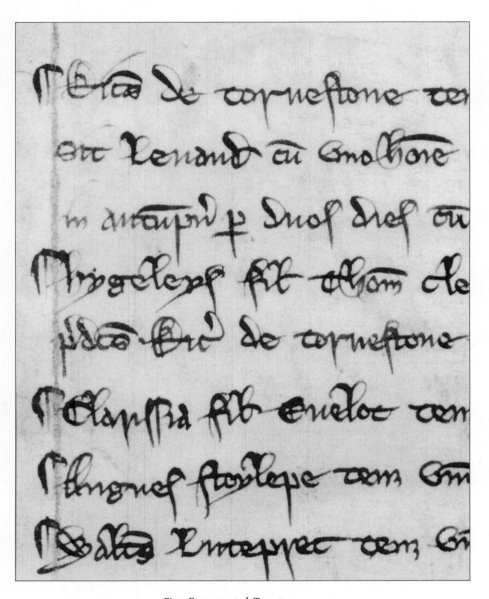

Fig.1. Errors averted: Turnstone
The letters n *and* u *may be indistinguishable in medieval hands, as in Richard 'de toruestone' in this manorial survey of 1297–8, lines 1 and 5. His family's name was Turweston, a Buckinghamshire place-name, but it had been read as Turnstone until a lucky chance corrected this just before the records naming them were published.*
Merton College, Oxford, Muniments 5899 (Man.Rec.Cux., p.111)

this kind really have virus-like qualities – error begets further error. If – which God forbid! – Turnstone finds its way into a reference book on surnames, anyone else finding Turuestone in a document and uncertain how to read it will be pleased to have the question answered and to have discovered another example of Turnstone. This then makes it the more likely that this is how a further person will read the name – and before long this non-existent name will have established itself as an interesting topographical surname, of limited regional distribution.

Just how appallingly easy it is to make mistakes of this sort, without any of the difficulties of medieval handwriting, can be shown by two instances of errors narrowly averted in volumes of eighteenth-century Portsmouth records. One was in Mr G. Hampson's edition of Customs letter-books, which refers to an extraordinary range of imported goods, many of them – especially the various types of Indian cloth – with strange names, some unknown to the *Oxford English Dictionary*: byrampaut, mendes holland, and others. Among them was a kind of wine or spirits, sange's, and at first there seemed to be another: the purser of HMS *Assurance* had a butt of what both the editor and I read as 'sonier' allowance wine. The manuscript is in a clear copperplate hand and there is no damage at that point. It was only after search had failed to produce any parallel or definition of the word for the glossary – but, after all, a search for sange's had failed – that light suddenly dawned. The hand of the letter-book wrote *w* exactly as *ni*, though without the dot: the word was really 'sower', sour (fig.2).[4] Soon after the volume had been published the editors of the new edition of the *Oxford English Dictionary*, now in preparation, appealed for news of hitherto unrecorded words; I responded by sending them copies of the glossaries from all the Portsmouth Record Series volumes. If sonier wine had not been stopped in time, it would now be well on the way to joining Lucy Toulmin Smith's additions to the English language.

The other instance narrowly missed adding a non-existent ship to the Royal Navy. It occurred in the volume of Marine Corps records, edited by Mr J.A. Lowe, among them the Portsmouth Division's earliest surviving book of daily orders, a journal of each day's events. Many of the entries record promotions or the embarcation of small detachments of marines on such-and-such a ship; very occasionally a blank has been left in place of the ship's name, 'H.M.S.   ', or just 'the   '. The entry on 19 December 1799, however, was quite clear: Private John Saunders of the 90th Company was appointed corporal in the *Eratta*. Ships' names are entered in the index with modern spelling, so I found myself searching for the normal form of what I thought might be a little-known Greek goddess, or a minor station in the Tropics – either might easily have provided a ship's name at this period. It was again only after nothing could be discovered that the truth appeared. For once the writer had failed

4   PthRS, 8, p.62.

Fig. 2. Errors averted: sonier wine

In editing this record 'Sower' in line 2 was read as 'Sonier', and it was only at the proof stage, after prolonged search had failed to find a wine so called, that the word was recognised as sour: a butt of sour allowance wine. In this hand w is sometimes, as in 'Allowance', written like ni, though without the dot.

PRO CUST 58/1, 29 December 1748 (PthRS, 8, p.62)

to leave a blank when he did not know the name of the ship, and 'Eratta' was the first word of the next entry, the only entry of its kind in the book: 'Eratta. In the Orders of the 17th December For Relieving Officer. Read. Relieved' (fig.3). Members of the board of the series were so moved by the abortive voyage of HMS *Eratta* that they persuaded me to write a short note on it for the *Mariner's Mirror*, to show just how easily this sort of mistake can occur.[5]

The Turnstone family, sonier wine and HMS *Eratta* were all saved only at the last minute from appearing in editions that historians and others would, quite properly, treat as primary sources. It is salutary to reflect that these same works – and any record text, despite all care – may include similar errors that escaped detection. Then, again, the process of printing can introduce new errors, independent of editor and general editor. When printing from the author's own disks first came in, it seemed as though halcyon days had arrived, the era of tedious proof-reading at last at an end – would it were so! We soon learned that setting from disks produced errors all its own, different, to be sure, from those produced by rekeying and, in fairness, normally fewer, but demanding just the same minute checking of proofs as before. A printer's error in the published text is no less harmful than a mistaken reading, and the same care is needed to avoid it. This includes checking by both editor and general editor: it cannot be said too often that a second eye will always see things that the first misses. I am lucky in having a good eye for correcting proofs, perhaps through being shortsighted, and in checking a text as general editor I sometimes find thirty or forty errors for every dozen spotted by the text's editor. But I am saved from any temptation to the sin of pride, for that dozen will always include some – often very obvious ones – that I have overlooked. Perfect proof-reading is not beyond the wit of man; we take for granted that it will be achieved in, say, Bibles and prayer-books. But to achieve it means that it must be done as thoroughly and carefully as every other part of the operation.

Accuracy, then, must not be seen as a mere ideal, unattainable in practice. If there is no hope of achieving it, it is better not to edit at all, for in producing an edition the editor is implicitly asking the user to trust its accuracy. No editor inspires confidence by putting '(*sic*)' after any word or phrase that looks odd; at best it is an admission of defeat, at worst a statement of incompetence, for what it says is 'I know there are mistakes in this text; it just happens that this isn't one of them'. Accuracy can be attained, but it will not come of itself: it calls for hard work, a great deal of time and patience, and great vigilance. It matters more than anything else.

5   PthRS, 7, p.109; P.D.A. Harvey, 'A ghost ship sunk', *Mariner's Mirror*, 78 (1992), p.201.

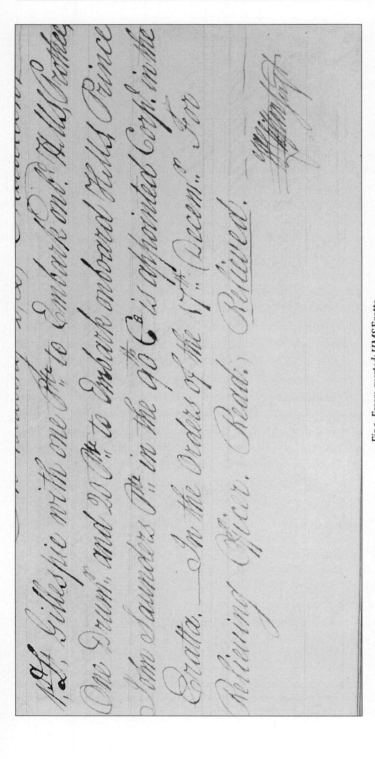

Fig.3. *Errors averted: HMS* Eratta

In these daily orders for the Portsmouth Division of Marines, 19 December 1799, it seems clear in lines 3 and 4 that the ship on which John Saunders has been appointed corporal is the Eratta. In fact his ship's name is left out and 'Eratta' introduces the following entry, correcting an order of two days earlier; realisation came only when the edited text was being indexed.

Portsmouth City Records Office 11A/23/5, f.172 (PthRS, 7, p.109)

Normalisation

It matters even more than the second rule of editing which underlies the rest of this chapter. It is only slightly less succinct than the first:

Say what you are going to do, and do it.

In other words, it does not so much matter what conventions one adopts in editing or calendaring – though some, to be sure, are to be preferred to others. What really matters is to say clearly what these conventions are, and then follow them through thick and thin with ruthless, even mindless, consistency. Even the omission of passages deemed improper – now surely a thing of the past – can be accepted as long as it is acknowledged that this has been done, as has not always been the case.[6] Taking this as an introduction, let us look at some of the possible options, first in full editing, then in calendaring.

In editing a document it is a good principle to let the editor intervene as little as possible between the original manuscript and the printed page: the text should follow the manuscript as closely as it can. However, even if this principle is adopted, it cannot be applied without reservation. An edition is not a facsimile. Typography is necessarily governed by disciplined constraints in its letter-forms, its lineation and its layout, whereas the original record need admit none of these limitations. To take a very simple example, normal printing offers two kinds of letter, upper-case or lower-case: capital or small. Many writers of records, however, use more than two: one kind for the letter that starts a sentence, for instance, another for the initial letters of proper nouns or other important words, and a third for other occasions (see fig.4). Some normalisation, then, is unavoidable, simply to bring the text within the confines of typography, and we look here at some of the ways the text itself may be normalised, leaving to the next chapter the question of layout on the manuscript and on the printed page. In some respects the edition is bound to tell us less than the facsimile does: we necessarily lose what a photocopy instantly shows us of the letter-forms, the tiny changes in the hand as the writer comes to the end of a page or of a day's work, the nuances of word spacing and so on. Every step we make in adapting, normalising, the text means that we lose more and more of the information that the facsimile would give us, and we have to be very sure that each step in this direction offers adequate compensation by way of improved access to the text, clearer understanding of its meaning, greater ease of reading it. Nor, indeed, is it just a matter of quantifiable information: every change means a change in the impression that the document makes on us, a loss of what is often called the flavour of the original. If

6   The consequent falsification of the historical record is discussed by J. Black, 'The language of licentiousness', *The Scriblerian and the Kit-Cats*, 26 (1994), p.153–9.

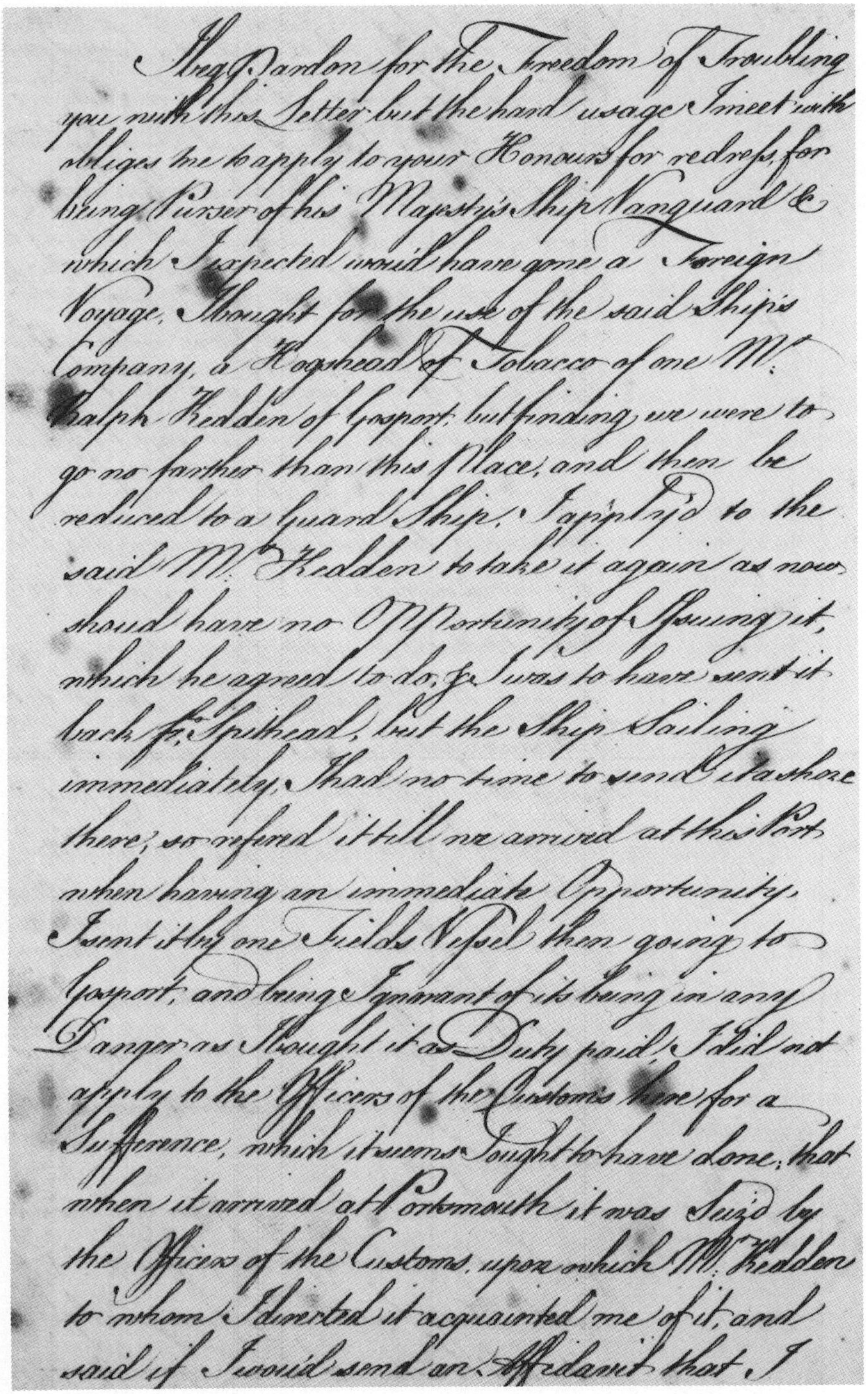

I beg Pardon for the Freedom of Troubling
you with this Letter but the hard usage I meet with
obliges me to apply to your Honours for redress, for
being Purser of his Majesty's Ship Vanguard &c
which I expected would have gone a Foreign
Voyage, I bought for the use of the said Ship's
Company, a Hogshead of Tobacco of one Mr.
Ralph Hedden of Gosport, but finding we were to
go no farther than this Place, and then be
reduced to a Guard Ship; I apply'd to the
said Mr. Hedden to take it again as now
should have no OPPortunity of Issuing it,
which he agreed to do, & I was to have sent it
back fr. Spithead, but the Ship Sailing
immediately, I had no time to send it ashore
there; so referd it till we arrived at this Port
when having an immediate Opportunity
I sent it by one Fields Vessel then going to
Gosport, and being Ignorant of its being in any
Danger as I bought it as Duty paid, I did not
apply to the Officers of the Customs here for a
Sufferance, which it seems I ought to have done; that
when it arrived at Portsmouth it was Seiz'd by
the Officers of the Customs, upon which Mr. Hedden
to whom I directed it acquainted me of it, and
said if I would send an Affidavit that I

Fig.4. Problems in transcribing the text

Even a clear copperplate hand of 1748 can pose problems in transcription. Does place *in line 9 have a capital initial? – its form differs from the* P *in either line 1 or line 4. If so, should* opportunity *in line 12 be transcribed as 'OPPortunity'? – it differs significantly from the same word in line 17.*

PRO CUST 58/149, p.88 (PthRS, 8, pp.35–6)

overall, taking notes and index into account, we have lost more than we have gained, so that the edition tells or shows us less than a photocopy would, then there is little point in the edition.

We have already looked at the thorny question of translating Latin records into English and have seen that, although it represents a massive editorial interposition between manuscript and printed page, the loss this represents can often be justified in making generally available texts that would otherwise be effectively inaccessible. Some other practices can be passed over briefly. No one today, I think, would follow what now seems the extraordinary convention of the Rolls Series, in both narrative and record texts, of converting their medieval Latin spelling into that of classical Latin – *aecclesia* for *ecclesia* and so on. Again, modernisation of medieval or early modern English spelling can seldom be justified; it is no way analogous with the translation of texts in Latin. There seems, for instance, little reason for it in the published volumes of Warwickshire quarter sessions records from 1625 on; with minimal gain in readability it distances the reader from the seventeenth-century text.[7] When a record such as an early account contains a great many roman numerals, some editors convert them to arabic ones. It certainly makes them easier to read, even for the specialist – there can be few today who find roman numerals easier, as Lord Burghley did in the sixteenth century. On the other hand we might say that there is a considerable loss of flavour, and the practice conceals the places in the text where the writers were most likely to have made mistakes; we can see at once that vij and viij are easily confused, whereas viij and ix are not, a point less obvious when they are written 7, 8, 9. But in all these cases what is done is no more than a question of style; all that matters is that the ways the manuscript's text has been adapted should be clearly stated and followed consistently. The reader should never be allowed to suppose that a particular spelling or other detail is copied from the manuscript, has contemporary authority, when really it is the editor's normalisation. Exactly the same applies to the questions to be discussed at greater length: punctuation, word division, letter forms and abbreviations.

There may be a strong temptation to normalise punctuation. Confronted with a late-medieval deed with erratically placed full stops and no commas, a seventeenth-century list of names with dashes and dots all over the place, a Victorian letter written as a stream of consciousness with virtually no punctuation at all, the editor may reasonably see it as a duty owed to the reader to adjust the punctuation to produce readable, structured prose or a nice, tidy list. The temptation should be resisted as far as possible; any regrets I have on this point as an editor all come from having normalised too much rather than too little. Normalising will always produce significant

---

7   *Quarter Sessions Order Book Easter, 1625, to Trinity, 1637*, ed. S.C. Ratcliff and H.C. Johnson (Warwick County Records, 1; 1935), and subsequent volumes.

loss. To imply, however involuntarily, that the list was compiled neatly and carefully, that the letter was a controlled composition, is to falsify the record. Sometimes a
text is punctuated more systematically than appears at first sight. Most early
medieval charters are clearly and regularly punctuated, though on a system different
from ours. In the Portsmouth Customs letter-books of 1748–50 the principal writer's
use of the apostrophe, at first indiscriminately before any terminal *s*, latterly more
sparingly, is of real interest, coming from the time when the use of the apostrophe to
mark the possessive was gaining ground.[8] Punctuation, more than anything else,
shows how writers thought about their writing and can thus be seen as a crucial part
of the record. One way of helping readers without introducing new punctuation is to
use extra spacing, now, with disk setting, achieved more easily than before: a double
space for a non-existent comma, for instance, or a triple space where a sentence ends
without a full stop.

However, the editor may find the temptation to normalise punctuation irre-
sistible. It is not just that modern readers are set in their ways and expect to have a
full stop at the end of a sentence. Some documents pose real problems. The royal
charter of 1682 to the borough of Portsmouth is some 10,000 words long, about a
quarter the length of this book. It is written as a single paragraph and, if we assume
no sentence starts with a conjunction, the body of the text consists of only fourteen
enormous sentences, with little help from full stops or commas. Here the gain in
introducing normal modern punctuation – making it clear that this had been done –
seemed far greater than any loss of flavour, or of providing a reliable source for the
development of punctuation in the seventeenth century.[9] But if they do normalise
punctuation in this way, editors must be certain they have read the text correctly. An
awful example of what can go wrong is a document, letters patent of Edward III, published at a time when one should have been able to trust the editor's Latin. It is not a
long document, some 400 words, but the body of the text is a single sentence of
some complexity, including, twice, a subordinate clause within a subordinate clause
within a subordinate clause. The editor has not aided comprehension in the least by
adding punctuation that includes two semi-colons and a full stop, one of the semi-
colons being right in the middle of one of the most subordinate clauses – in fact the
document has been turned into a meaningless muddle, and the only way it can be
understood is to ignore all the editor's punctuation and start again.[10] If punctuation
is introduced into sentences of this complexity, it can be helpful to resort to round
brackets, not just commas, to lay bare their structure.

8   PthRS, 8.
9   PthRS, 9, pp.60–95.
10   *The Cartulary and Terrier of the Priory of Bilsington, Kent*, ed. N. Neilson (Brit.Ac., RSEH, old series 7;
     1928), pp.213–14.

Some particularly tricky points of punctuation are best looked at later: the full stops and apostrophes used as marks of abbreviation and the hyphen used to break a word at the end of a line, as well as the full stop omitted when a sentence ends there. Something should be said here, though, about word division, a minor problem that affects some records of all periods. In medieval records we sometimes find preposition and noun written together as a single word – *perplegium* in naming a surety, *intermino* in giving a date – or, more rarely, a word's prefix separated from it as though it were an independent adverb or preposition – *in iuste* for *iniuste*, meaning wrongly.[11] In many later texts, as indeed in modern orthography, there is doubt whether a particular combination should be written as two words or as one, and we sometimes find what we see as single words written as two: 'an other', 'a part', 'high way', 'turn pike' are eighteenth-century examples. There seems no reason to impose normalisation on these forms; there is seldom any problem of comprehension and, like the punctuation, they offer a sidelight on the writer's way of thought. There may even be risk in normalisation, and though few of us will find ourselves editing Old English texts containing words otherwise unknown, it is worth bearing in mind the experience of so skilled and careful an editor as Felix Liebermann when he edited the supposed semi-legal text *Gerefa*. In normalising the punctuation and the often eccentric word division of the unique manuscript of about 1100 he merely added a further layer of obscurity to what was in parts already a difficult text.[12]

If punctuation is normalised, logic demands the normalisation of capital letters too – a capital letter to introduce a sentence or a proper noun and nowhere else – and in medieval texts especially this can be very helpful to the reader. But if punctuation is not normalised – and I think this is the better course – there is no reason to normalise capital letters and, indeed, their incidence can be of real interest, even if they occur in the middle of a word. That a clerk in 1295 wrote a surname as 'WaldRugge' tells us something of the way he perceived the name; that another in 1748 occasionally wrote 'OPPortunity' and 'OPinion' in mid-sentence, though no more than a personal quirk, is still evidence of habits of mind and of script.[13] What to do, then, if the manuscript uses more than one level of capital letter, one for the start of a sentence, another for names or whatever? We cannot reproduce these nuances on the printed page. Probably the best solution is to print as a capital any letter that is not in small, lower-case, form in the manuscript. This makes the point that they are different from the rest and if, as it should, the edition includes reproductions of pages of the

11   *Man.Rec.Cux.*, pp.699, 122; 614.
12   R.I. Page, '"The proper toil of artless industry": Toronto's plan for an Old English dictionary', *Notes and Queries*, 220 (1975), pp.148–9; R.I. Page, 'Gerefa: some problems of meaning', in *Problems of Old English Lexicography: Studies in Memory of Angus Cameron*, ed. A. Bammesberger (Regensburg, 1985), pp.217–19.
13   *Man.Rec.Cux.*, p.612; PthRS, 8, pp.35, 36.

manuscript, these will give some indication of the original's range of letter-forms.

Otherwise, the letter-forms used in the manuscript ought to give no difficulty. An edition is not a facsimile, and its basis is to use the modern printed letters that correspond to the letters of the manuscript, without regard to the style of handwriting or the particular letter forms favoured by the writer. If a particular hand writes capital *F* as *ff*, it is as *F* that it appears in the edition. In fact, however, two problems arise. The first is in medieval texts. Writers in the middle ages, as in all later periods, often wrote particular letters in more than one form: a long and a 2-shaped *r*, for instance, or a short and a long *s*. Very commonly *u* was written not only in the rounded form but also (especially at the beginning of a word) with a pointed foot, and *i* not only in the short form but also (especially at the end of a word) with a long descender. Because these forms – pointed *u*, long *i* – have the appearance of the modern letters *v* and *j*, editors have often reproduced them thus when they occur in the manuscript, though it was only in the mid-seventeenth century that they began to be used exclusively for these consonants. In 1925 Sir Henry Maxwell Lyte published a short, cogent note saying that there was no justification for this practice, which he found 'neither correct nor pleasing', and urging editors to normalise the use of these letter forms.[14] His logic is unassailable, yet to this day many editors, myself included, have persisted in reproducing the manuscripts' use of short and long *i*, round and pointed *u*. Why? I see several reasons. The long *i* at the end of a word or, especially, a numeral can help the reader of the printed text just as it was meant to help the reader of the manuscript: it is easier to distinguish between iij and iiij than between iii and iiii. The rounded *u* in most medieval hands is indistinguishable from *n* but there is no risk of confusion when the pointed form is used; if the name of the Turweston family of Cuxham had, even only once, been written with the pointed *u*, as 'Turvestone', the Turnstones would never have come into existence. To anyone using the printed text, aware of the ambiguity between *u* and *n*, it can be useful to know if the pointed form of *u* occurs, as it can dispel any doubts over the correctness of the editor's reading. Admittedly the same argument could be used to reproduce the manuscript's long and short forms of *s*, as there can sometimes be real confusion between the long *s* and *f*. But – and this I see as the crucial point – the alternative forms of *u* and *i* are not analogous with the alternative forms of *s* or of any other letter. It is not irrelevant that the pointed *v*, the long *j*, came in both English and French to represent separate sounds, to be separate letters in their own right. To normalise them in vernacular texts would be to obscure important developments in speech and orthography, and though these developments did not occur in written Latin, there are few record texts that include no words at all in the vernacular, if only the

14   H. Maxwell Lyte, '"U" and "V": a note on palaeography', *Bulletin of the Institute of Historical Research*, 2 (1924–5), pp.63–5.

names of persons and places. There is a better case for retaining the alternative forms of *u* and *i* in the printed text than Maxwell Lyte would allow.

The second problem over letter-forms is in early-modern texts: the use of *y* in place of *th*. Historically the *y* in the definite article 'ye' and the *y* in 'your' are quite different letters; the th-*y* developed as an alternative to the runic letter thorn, Þ. The replacement of Þ by *y*, with some confusion between the two letters, began in the late fourteenth century in northern and eastern England,[15] and by the sixteenth century *y* was the only alternative to *th*, whether in print or in manuscript. To make a distinction in the modern edition where it was not made in the record, using some form of Þ for the th-*y* or normalising it to *th*, would be, as Maxwell Lyte would say, neither correct nor pleasing, though it might usefully remind the non-specialist reader how the th-*y* was actually pronounced. Difficulties over the th-*y* arise mostly in the last phase of its use, in the late seventeenth and eighteenth centuries, when it was seen as not a letter so much as a part of a standard abbreviation, like an ampersand, &: the following letter would normally be superscript, as 'y^e', 'y^t'. The writer of 'y^t', asked to spell the word out in full, would at this date put 'that', seeing 'yat' as an archaic absurdity. It is as standard abbreviations that they are best treated in printed editions. Like &, the form 'y^e' should give the modern reader no difficulty and there seems no reason to change it in editing; but it is arguably more correct to, as it were, expand the abbreviation to 'the' than to lower the *e* to make 'ye', and if 'y^t' is thought to stand in the way of easy reading, the only possible expansion is 'that'. This leads us into the whole question of abbreviations in the manuscript, often the hardest of all the problems that confront an editor.

Abbreviations

It is a problem that affects records of all periods, but it is most acute in medieval texts written in Latin, so it is best to start with them and then see how far the principles involved can be applied to later documents. When R.E. Latham commented that of British texts in medieval Latin 'few have been edited with anything like the care normally expended on Classical or even Middle English texts' he will have had misreadings in mind to be sure, but probably above all the faulty extension of the manuscripts' abbreviations.[16] Just how easy it is to fall into error is brought home by two discussions of common words: C.R. Cheney has queried whether *quum* as a form of *cum* really exists or whether it is not always a false extension of the abbreviation

---

15   M. Benskin, 'The letters <Þ> and <y> in later Middle English and some related matters', *Journal of the Society of Archivists*, 7 (1982–5), pp. 13–30. I am grateful to Dr A.I. Doyle for telling me of this article.

16   *Revised Medieval Latin Word-List from British and Irish Sources*, ed. R.E. Latham (London, 1965), p.ix.

for *quoniam*, and Dr Pierre Chaplais has argued that the standard abbreviation *xps* with a line above should properly be extended not to *Christus* but to *Cristus*.[17] As a rule the authors of scholarly editions of medieval works in English will show which words have been abbreviated in the manuscript, usually by putting any supplied letters in italic. In writing Latin in the middle ages far more abbreviations were used than in writing English, and generally records were more heavily abbreviated than literary texts; there was much use of familiar words and formulas and it is not uncommon to find records where every other word is an abbreviation. To supply all missing letters in italics would produce an unsightly text, which would be extremely difficult to print accurately. Confronted with this problem, editors have devised two extreme solutions that have been commonly used over the past two hundred years. Both are born of despair, for neither really faces up to the difficulties.

One is to use record type. This was devised in the 1770s for Abraham Farley's edition of Domesday Book. Special type was designed by John Nichols to reproduce in print all the abbreviations and letter forms that occur in the manuscript: a *p* with a loop through the descender, a 2-shaped *r* with a vertical stroke, a zigzag sign above a letter, and so on (fig.5). This removed the problem entirely, for the editor offered no view as to what the particular abbreviation stood for, how a word should be extended: this was left to the reader, who may thus have been given no help but who at least ran no risk of being misled. Record type was used for quite a number of editions of medieval documents in the nineteenth century, but gradually fell from favour; its last foothold seems to have been the Pipe Roll Society, which finally abandoned its use in 1904.[18] Although clumsy, it is not an inefficient method of transcription: the abbreviations in the manuscript are nearly always precisely written and it is perfectly feasible to reproduce the text in this way. It eliminates as far as possible the intrusion of the editor between document and reader. However, it effectively confines its readership to those with a knowledge not just of Latin but of palaeography as well, and any reader might feel entitled to rather more help from the edition than it can offer. Once photographic techniques became generally available it fell badly between two stools, giving less than a facsimile on the one hand, less than an extended text on the other. All the same, it would be wrong to underestimate the virtues of record type. Although it simply evades the difficulty of abbreviations, at least it does

17 C.R. Cheney, '*Quum* and *quoniam*', *Bulletin of the Institute of Historical Research*, 24 (1951), pp.44–5; P. Chaplais, 'The spelling of Christ's name in medieval Anglo-Latin: "Christus" or "Cristus"?', *Journal of the Society of Archivists*, 8 (1986–7), p.261–76.

18 *The Great Roll of the Pipe for the Twenty-Second Year of the Reign of King Henry the Second* (Pipe Roll Society, old series 25; 1904) notes in the preface, p.vii, that 'The Roll is printed, as resolved by the General Meeting, *in extenso*, instead of in Record type, as hitherto', and then, very properly, sets out the 'Rules for Copying' that are to be followed in future.

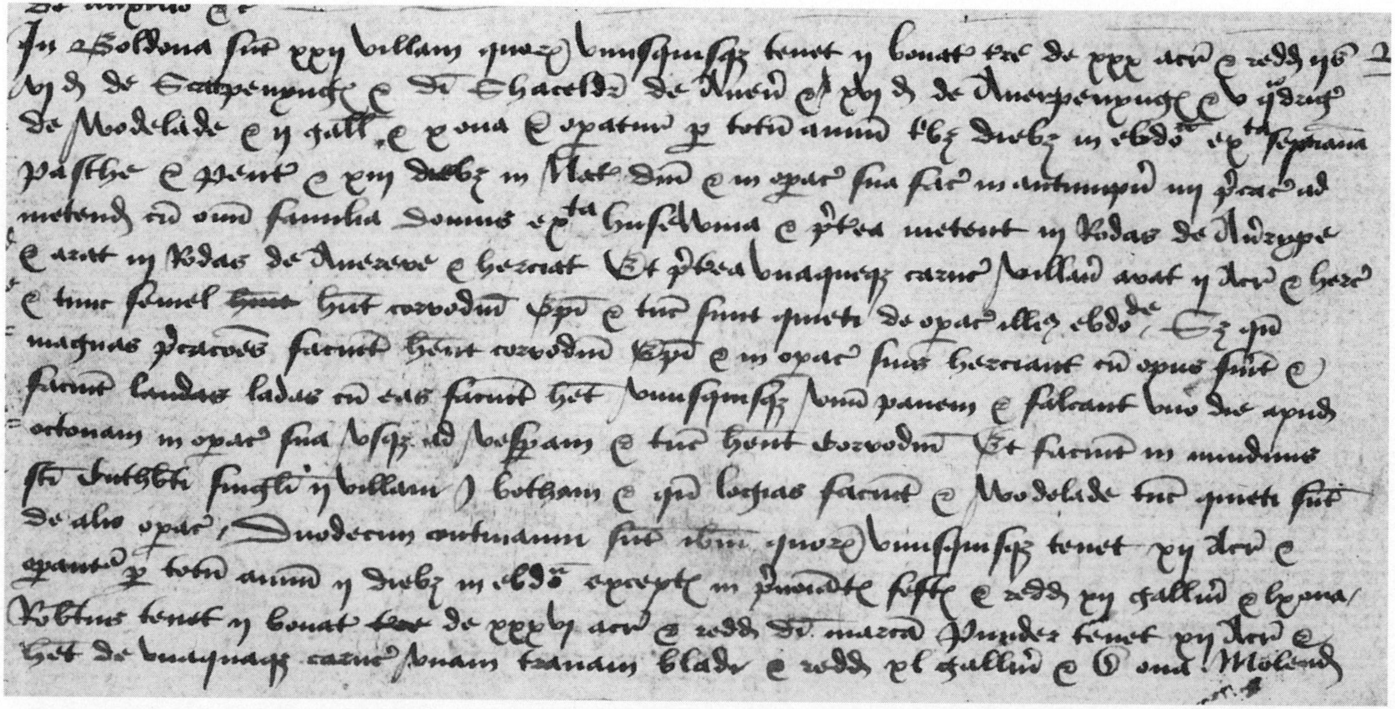

Fig. 5. Record type

Comparing this passage of printed text with the fifteenth-century manuscript of the Boldon Book, the bishop of Durham's estate survey of 1183 or 1184, we see how specially made type accurately reproduces the abbreviations of the original, as in sunt, quorum, unusquisque, in the opening words. The result is not easy to read but it avoids any risk of misinterpretation; thus we see that 'gall' in line 3 may be either cocks (gallos) or hens (gallinas). The editor has, however, normalised the manuscript's round and pointed u, short and long i, while retaining its exact lineation.

Bodleian Library, Oxford, MS. Laud 542, f.1r; Libri censualis, vocati Domesday-book, additamenta, ed. [H. Ellis] (Record Commission, 1816), opp. p.[56]

In Boldona sūt xxii villani, quoȝ unufquifȝ tenet ii bovat' t're de xxx acr' & redđ. ii s. vi đ de Scatpenyng(& đi Shaceldr' de Aven' & xvi đ de Averpenyng(& v qdrig' de Wodelade & ii gatt & x ova, & opatur p totū annū tbȝ diebȝ in ebdo ex feptiāna Pafche & Pent' & xiii diebȝ in Nat' Dñi & in opac' fua fac' in Autumpn' iiii p'cac' ad metend cū oñi familia Domus ex Hufewiva : & p't'ea metunt iii Rodas de Av'ype, & arat iii. Rodas de Averere & herciat. Et p't'ea vnaquȝeȝ caruc' Villan' arat ii acᷓ & herᷓ. & tunc femel hīt corrodiū Ep̄i. & tūc funt quieti de opacᷓ illiᵒ ebdo. Sȝ qu' magnas p'cacͦoes faciūt hēnt corrodiū Ep̄i & in opac' fuis herciant, cū opus fu'it, & faciūt ladas : cū eas faciūt het unufquifȝ unū panem ; & falcant uno die apud octonam in opac' fua ufqȝ ad vefpam, & tūc hēnt Corrodiū. Et faciūt in nundinis sͮti Cuthbti fingti ii villani i botham ; & qũ logias faciūt & Wodelade tūc quieti sūt de alio opac. Duodecim cotmanni sūt ibm quoȝ unufquifȝ tenet xii Acr' & opant per totū annū ii diebȝ in ebdo except(in p'ñoiat(feft(& redđ xii gallin' & lx ova. Robtus tenet ii bovat de xxxvi acr' & redđ đi marcā. Punder tenet xii acr' & hēt de unaquaȝ caruc' unam travam bladi ; & redđ xl gallin' & D. ova Molenđ

no disservice to scholarship by getting things wrong, and it thus avoids the worst editorial sin of all.

The same cannot be said of the other desperate solution. This belongs firmly to what we have identified as the all-for-history style of editing historical texts: if the meaning is clear anything else is of minor importance. It consists of extending all abbreviations silently – that is, without showing that the words were abbreviated in the original – following, if in any doubt, the vocabulary and grammar of classical Latin, though not, except in the Rolls Series, its spelling (fig.6). The result is a clear text, easy to read, with all the difficulties of abbreviations done away with. The trouble is, though, that it can all too easily be wrong. Often a word is abbreviated every time it occurs in the manuscript; we may flatter the writer's latinity by supposing he used the classical form and extending it thus, but this can be no more than a guess. Or it may be a word unknown to classical Latin, in which case we can extend it only by seeing how it is spelled in other medieval texts; but their editors may have been less scrupulous than we and, finding it was never written out in full in their documents, have simply invented an ending for it. The early pipe rolls of the bishops of Winchester – their estate accounts – use a word for the profits of the local courts, unusual in this context, which the editors of the two thirteenth-century printed accounts give as *purchasia*. Now, however, Dr Katharine Stocks has found that in all the accounts down to 1250 the word is always abbreviated after the *h* – except once, when it is *p'chac'*.[19] How it ended we do not know, though *purchacia* is likely. But what we do now know is that these particular documents offer no support for spelling *purchasia* with an *s*: it is an editorial invention. Again, in classical Latin the noun following the preposition *super*, above, is in either the accusative case, if motion is involved, or in the ablative if it is not; in medieval documents the case is commonly concealed by abbreviating the end of the noun. In the Cuxham manorial records practically every time the noun after *super* is not abbreviated it is in the accusative case, whether or not motion is involved.[20] Because edited records silently extend the noun according to the classical rule, it is impossible to tell from them whether the Cuxham practice was or was not normal usage among those who wrote Latin records in the thirteenth and fourteenth centuries. What point is there in printing a text in Latin if it cannot be relied on as evidence for Latin usage? If the purpose of an edition is simply to present the text's meaning, why have it in Latin at all? Far better to have a translation in good English than a Latin text that perverts the language of the documents.

At which point one might succumb to the prevalent despair and decide that record type is the only acceptable alternative to an English translation. It is not as

19   K.J. Stocks, 'Manorial Courts in England before 1250' (Durham PhD thesis, 1998), pp.46–7.
20   *Man.Rec.Cux.*, p.797.

bad as that. To start with, even if every other word of the text is abbreviated, there can be no conceivable doubt over the correct extension of a great many of them. A *p* with a loop through the descender stands for *pro* just as unambiguously as if the word were written out; a 9-shaped sign at the end of a word can only mean *us*. A *p* with a simple stroke through the descender most often stands for *per*, but on occasion can also be *par, por* or *pur*; when it stands alone, however, it must be *per* and when, for instance, it occurs in *puus* we can safely extend the word to *paruus* – any alternative would be wholly eccentric, however unclassical the writer's Latin. A hook over a *t* has various possible meanings, but when it occurs in *tra* in an appropriate context the word is certainly *terra*. Thus even the most cautious editor can expand many abbreviations with complete confidence; one can scarcely allow that a subjective element has crept in, when any alternative extension would produce a hitherto unknown form of a common word. But one can easily go further than this. A writer may have normally abbreviated a word where there can be doubt over its full form – but occasionally, even just once, wrote it in fully or partly extended form, as happened with *p'chac'* in the Winchester pipe rolls. This permits us to extend the word every time it is abbreviated, though that this has been done should be noted in an appropriate list, along with a reference to the extended form in the manuscript. We must remember too that individual writers differed – we cannot take the way one writer extended the word as evidence for the way it would have been extended by another. Nor, indeed, for the way the same writer would have extended it every time – we cannot rely on complete consistency and, indeed, the fact of variation is itself of interest. Thus in the Cuxham manorial records, vetch is most often referred to in abbreviated form as *ves'*; one writer occasionally extends it to *vesse*, most of the others to *vesce*, but two of them to either form indiscriminately.[21] With a note that these extended forms occur in the manuscript there is no reason why the word should not be extended silently every time it occurs. The important thing, as always, is to state clearly what has been done.

By all these devices it is possible to reduce to an entirely acceptable minimum the italic signifying an editorial extension. The editor will probably find that a high proportion of the extensions that have to be italicised arise from uncertainty over the tense of a verb or whether a noun is singular or plural. At the time it was clear to both the writer and whoever read what he wrote whether there was, say, one mill in a village or more than one, so it was adequate to write *molend'* with no indication of singular or plural; but it is not so clear to us, and it sets one of the worst snares for anyone extending a text for publication. It has entrapped many editors, and as it is historical, not linguistic, information that is at stake, we can say that this is a point where the all-for-history style of editing can very easily let the historian down.

21   *Man.Rec.Cux.*, p.800.

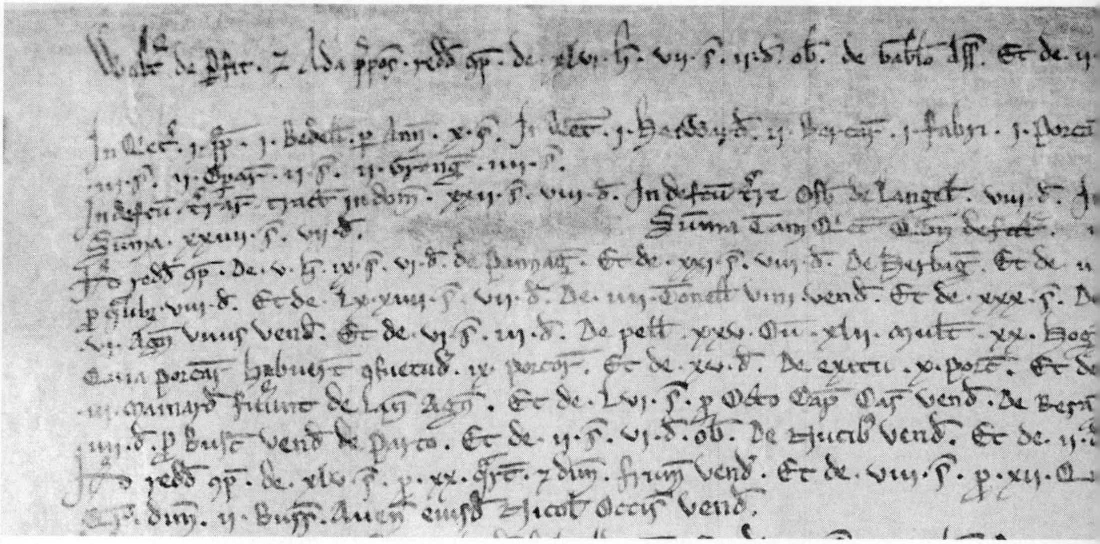

Fig. 6. All-for-history style

*These 1208–9 estate accounts of the bishop of Winchester are an example of an edited text that silent-
ly extends abbreviations to make acceptable Latin: the text's meaning is what matters and the language that conveys it is of secondary importance. It is not an extreme example, being specifically
based on 'close observation of the habits of the scribe', yet we may wonder whether even in this short
extract all the word-forms can be justified from any part of the manuscript. Can we be sure that the
writer used the plural 'In quietanciis' for acquittance of rent, the singular 'De reragio' for items
brought forward from the last account (manuscript 'Quiet''lines 3 etc., 'Rerag' line 11; printed text
lines 4 etc., 23); or that the accusative, not the ablative, was used in 'tractarum in dominium' ('tract'
in dom'' line 5; line 8)? The editor expresses doubt over extending 'Hogg'' to 'hoggettorum' (line 9; line
18); similar doubts arise over 'pullorum' for 'Pull'', which might stand for 'Pullanorum', or 'busca'
for 'Busc'', which might equally be 'Buscha', 'Buscia' or 'Buschia' (lines 8, 12; lines 17, 24). The editor
has normalised capital letters as well as the manuscript's round and pointed u, short and long i, and
has changed e to ae where demanded by classical Latin spelling.*

*Hampshire Record Office 11M59/B1/1, mem.1; The Pipe Roll of the Bishopric of Winchester,
1208–1209, ed. H. Hall (Studies in Economic and Political Science, 1903), p.1*

WALTERUS DE PARFIT et Adam præpositus reddunt compotum de xlvj*l.* vijs. ij*d. ob.* de gabulo assiso. Et de ijs. de Henrico villatæ de incremento gabuli de terra Bal. Et de ijs. de incremento gabuli Michaelis Hudi, pro viij acris.   Summa xlvj*l.* xjs. ij*d. ob.*

In quietanciis j præpositi, j bedelli, per annum, xs.   In quietanciis j haiwardi, ij bercariorum, j fabri, j porcarii, per annum, ixs. vj*d.*   In quietanciis vij carrucariorum, xiiijs.   In quietanciis x operariorum, xxs., j operarii cum biga sua, iijs., ij operariorum, ijs., ij grangiariorum, iiijs.   Summa lxijs. vj*d.*

In defectu terrarum tractarum in dominium, xxijs. viij*d.*   In defectu terræ Osberti de Langel[ega], viij*d.*   In defectu terræ Ricardi Baconis, vj*d.*   In defectu terræ Henrici filii Azonis, vj*d.*   In defectu terræ Walteri de Swanemere, iij*d.*   Summa xxiiijs. vij*d.*

[2] Summa tam quietanciarum quam defectuum, iiij*l.* vijs. j*d.*

Et remanent xlij*l.* iiijs. iij *ob.*

Idem reddunt compotum de vl. ixs. vj*d.* de pannagio.   Et de xxjs. viij*d.* de herbagio. Et de ijs. vj*d.* de junceo vendito.   Et de xviijs. de vj bobus vivis venditis.   Et de xxijs. de xxxiij ovibus vivis venditis, pro qualibet, viij*d.*   Et de lx.xiiijs. vij*d.* de iiij tonellis vini venditis.   Et de xxxs. de coreis xxix boum, v vaccarum, ij annalium, iiij equarum, iiij pullorum mortuorum venditis.   Et de xviij*d.* de vj [3] agnis vivis venditis.   Et de vjs. iij*d.* de pellibus xxv ovium, xlij multonum, xx hogg[ettorum].   Et de vjs. de pellibus iiij[xx].xj agnorum mortuorum venditis.   Et de xxviijs. de uncto ccxiij porcorum vendito, quia porcarius habuerat consuetudinem ix porcorum.   Et de xv*d.* de exitu x porcorum.   Et de ijs. de xl parvis caseis factis in hyeme.   Et de vij*l.* ixs. iiij*d.* de v ponderibus grossæ lanæ et agninæ, unde iij mainardi fuerunt de lana agnina.   Et de lvjs. pro octo capitibus casei venditis de reragio anni præteriti.   Et de vjs. x*d.* pro xlj acris locatis hoc anno, pro singula acra ij*d.*   Et de cvijs. iiij*d.* pro busca vendita de parco.   Et de ijs. vj*d. ob.* de nucibus venditis.   Et de ij*d. ob.* pro j galone mellis vendito.   Summa xxxij*l.* vjs. vj*d.*

Idem reddunt compotum de xlvs. pro xx quarteriis et dimidio frumenti venditis.   Et

This word-by-word method of extending abbreviations may sound laborious, and it does indeed call for slow, careful work, but if it is planned from the start it is not too difficult or time-consuming. It provides the editor with a valuable word-list, showing what usages really do have the authority of the manuscript, a firm basis for the work of lexicographers and of other editors. When I used the method for the Cuxham manorial records I saw it as experimental, and was delighted when Dr C.M. Woolgar adopted it in his far harder task of editing household accounts extending over some three hundred years, from the late twelfth century to the late fifteenth.[22] One drawback to the method is, of course, that it is not quite foolproof. In describing it in the introduction to the Cuxham documents I wrote that some abbreviations, though theoretically not unambiguous, could still be extended silently: 'where doubt over a particular extension would imply a perverse and otherwise unrecorded eccentricity on the part of the writer pedantry must be allowed to give way to common sense'. I had in mind the reasonable certainty one can have in cases such as *paruus* and *terra* – but whereas reasonable certainty can be fairly precisely defined, as I tried to do there, it cannot be defined absolutely, leaving a door ever so slightly ajar to the slippery slope that has at the bottom the all-for-history style, silently extending everything. One person's simple caution can be another person's pedantry, and it cannot be said too strongly that being over-pedantic is not a risk – here or indeed in any aspect of editing. Common sense – meaning, as often as not, the editor's own guesses – has been brought into play far too much in editing medieval Latin records in Britain, pedantry far too little. I do not know of a single medieval Latin record where there has been too much pedantry in editing; I know a great many where there has not been nearly enough, merely too much common sense.

Whatever method is followed, need every abbreviation be extended, whether silently or with italics? Probably not. In a text that refers to a great many sums of money, there seems little point in extending its *li'*, *s'*, *d'*, that is, pounds, shillings and pence, to *libre*, *solidi*, *denarii*; in fact it will be easier to read if they are left unabbreviated. It may even be convenient to introduce an editorial abbreviation for often recurring words – *bus.* for *bussellus*, bushel, in lists of corn, for instance. Here again, all that matters is to make clear that this has been done, and ideally note the actual usage of the manuscript. But how far we should retain the abbreviations of the text is a question that looms much larger in post-medieval records in English than in medieval Latin ones.

We have spent a long time looking at the problem of abbreviations in medieval

---

22 *Household Accounts from Medieval England*, ed. C.M. Woolgar (Brit.Ac., RSEH, new series 17, 18; 1992–3), i, pp.71–104.

Latin records because it is a peculiarly difficult one, indeed by far the most difficult that the editor of these texts is likely to face. But abbreviations in texts in English, from the late middle ages on, pose problems too, though they are less intractable. This is largely because, almost always, far fewer words are abbreviated in English than in Latin texts and there is generally less room for doubt over what the missing letters are likely to be. In any case, because there are fewer abbreviations there is not the same difficulty in using italic to supply all these missing letters, so no violence need be done to linguistic scholarship. All the same, English texts can sometimes produce harder conundrums than one commonly finds in the Latin: in a mid-eighteenth-century list of stationery, for instance, is 'V.B.' to be read as '*V*at B*lued*' or as '*V*ellum *B*ound' or as neither?[23]

But although all abbreviations may be extended in italic in a way that is simply not practicable in medieval Latin texts, in some records where certain abbreviations often recur this can still leave one with a fearful amount of italic, difficult to check and distracting to the reader; it even verges on absurdity to put 'w*hich*', 'w*ith*' every time if 'w^{ch}', 'wth', is how they are normally written in the record. But it is words occurring frequently in the document that are most often abbreviated. This means that a great many italic letters can be avoided by the simple device of compiling a list of abbreviations that will always be extended silently in the particular edition. If, of course, a word is abbreviated in a different way on one or two occasions, italics should be used; but in the eighteenth-century Portsmouth texts that have been published a list of from one to two dozen commonly abbreviated words for silent extension reduced the amount of italic needed to no more than an occasional expedient, an entirely acceptable level, while doing no violence to the study of linguistics or orthography. When an abbreviation is extended one naturally omits any sign of abbreviation, such as a line above the word or superscript letters: 'wth' becomes 'with', not 'with'. This includes the full stop: in post-medieval English texts it is nearly always clear whether the stop is simply a mark of abbreviation or whether it has independent status in serving also as a mark of punctuation, though in medieval texts, English or Latin, it can sometimes be harder to decide.

In post-medieval English texts there will often be many abbreviations best left unextended. Clearly 'Mr.' and 'Mrs.' should be left – in the early eighteenth century, after all, the recipient of a letter may himself not have known whether his correspondent intended 'Mister' or 'Master' – and a host of other abbreviations that, with minor variation, are in common use now as they have been for centuries: the months of the year, military ranks, 'no.', 'viz.', and many more. As they are familiar to the readers they will not impede easy reading and they do much to convey the

23 PthRS, 8, pp.74, 160, 204.

general impression, the flavour, of the original manuscript. Nor is there any reason to normalise them: 'Genl' is as comprehensible as 'Genl.', while 'Col^{l}' is rather more comprehensible than 'Coll.' or even 'Col'l'. Three details of experience at Portsmouth seem worth mentioning. In our only fully edited texts with frequent references to military ranks, the Marine Corps records of 1764–1800, it seemed sensible to align with modern usage in retaining the abbreviations before a name, while extending it in other contexts: 'Serj^{t} Dowling' as in the manuscript, but 'One Serjeant and 3 Privates' where the manuscript has 'One Serj^{t} and 3 P^{tes}'.[24] Second, whether this is a quirk of the particular texts we have published or a significant clue to orthographical development, it has worked well to leave unextended any abbreviation made with an apostrophe, again a familiar modern usage. The third is that we omit any punctuation – full stop, comma, hyphen – below superscript letters in abbreviations that are retained, for a wholly pragmatic reason: the difficulty of reproducing them in several of the successive techniques used for setting the volumes.

Calendars

The calendar, a carefully controlled, rigorously consistent précis, offers many advantages where there is no compelling reason for publishing the full text, especially, as we have seen, where there is easy access to the original records or to cheap photocopies. By giving the gist of the record, omitting common form and unnecessary verbiage, the calendar on one hand presents records more compactly – more in the same space – than a full edition, and often in a more accessible form; and on the other hand, unlike a catalogue or an index, it provides most readers with all the information they need, without recourse to the original record. However, we must acknowledge from the start that the calendar runs risks that both the full edition and the catalogue avoid, risks that the editor may all too easily fail to recognise. A 1333 entry in the *Calendar of Patent Rolls* illustrates this neatly. The bishop of Lincoln had claimed that certain men had (according to the calendar) 'at divers times imprisoned at Cruche by Bannebury' merchants coming to his fair and market at Banbury. We might take this as evidence that Crouch Hill, just outside Banbury, was then the site of a settlement, or at least gave its name to a substantial house. But if we look at the patent roll itself, we see that it tells us nothing of the sort: the alleged wrongdoers (retaining the word order of the Latin text) 'at Cruche by Bannebury at divers times took and imprisoned' the unfortunate merchants.[25] What happened at Crouch Hill

24   PthRS, 7, p.119.
25   *Calendar of Patent Rolls, 1330–4*, p.499; PRO, C 66/182, m.23d.

was certainly their seizure, which is entirely plausible, but not necessarily their imprisonment, which would be a good deal more surprising. The calendar here has subtly and unconsciously altered the sense of the record. It needs the greatest care to avoid mistakes like this.

Indeed, it cannot be said too emphatically that calendaring is not the soft option that editors have sometimes assumed: paraphrasing the text without the need for the tediously minute accuracy that a full edition calls for in every word. Calendaring is significantly harder than straightforward editing. It is not just a matter of avoiding the mistakes produced by overlooking the nuances of the manuscript. It demands a degree of consistency that can be quite difficult to achieve. If two entries in a calendar are identical in form and structure the reader should not suppose that the documents themselves are similarly identical: there may be differences between them that the editor, quite properly, has decided are unimportant, so that there is no need to bring them out in the calendar entries. But if two calendar entries differ in form or structure, the reader is entitled to assume that this reflects actual differences in the documents themselves, differences that the editor sees as significant. Obviously enough, what information is included and what is omitted in each entry must be consistent throughout the calendar. It is less obvious, but scarcely less important, that the way this information is presented, its ordering and its phrasing, should be equally consistent, so that any variation arises from variations in the documents themselves, not from editorial vagaries.

What in fact should be included in a calendar and what omitted? A helpful yardstick in deciding is to consider what would be indexed if the document were published in full – all names of persons and places, all material objects, certain abstract procedures and concepts, for instance. Then, perhaps, one might decide that the calendar must include all these, so that the index is as complete as if the documents had been fully edited; or perhaps all these, and some other specified detail as well; or perhaps certain classes of indexable information are to be omitted. This is offered only as a method of defining what to include in a calendar, not as any kind of advice as to what ought or ought not to be put in. For this there can be no general guidance. Calendaring covers a wide range of précis writing, from what is little more than an expanded catalogue entry to what falls little short of a full edition. What level of calendaring is appropriate for any group of records depends on the general policy and particular strategy of their publication. Nor need there be consistency in the level of calendaring between different classes of record in a single volume. In the Portsmouth volume of adult-education records Edwin Welch gave very full detail from the class registers and from the correspondence on each course preserved in the university board's letter-books, but for the printed syllabus issued for each course it seemed sufficient to give bibliographical details and the title of each lecture. However, one syllabus was included in an appendix giving the full text of specimen documents – we chose the syllabus for H.E. Malden's course in 1901 on the history of Hampshire which, having covered all the ground from the Stone Age to the siege of Portsmouth in 1659, ended there with the remarkable comment that this was 'The end of eventful history'.[26] It is a good principle to print the full text of a specimen of each kind of document calendared in a volume; following the rule of saying what has been done, it shows more clearly than any descriptive text just what level of calendaring has been applied and what more can be learned by consulting the original documents.

Some texts do not submit easily to calendaring. Dr Roger Knight met this problem in his volume of Portsmouth dockyard papers. At first sight the correspondence of 1774–83 seemed verbose, full of polite flourishes, but once one had stripped away these flourishes – 'We are Honourable Sirs Your most obedient Servants' and so on – one was left with a dense and efficient business letter, with no words wasted.[27] If one finds oneself paraphrasing all or part of the original without reducing its length, there is no point in the paraphrase; it is better to give the relevant text in full in quotation marks, thus giving the reader the benefit of the document's actual wording. There will nearly always be points in a calendar where quotation from the original is called for, either because the passage is as succinct as any paraphrase or simply because it seems particularly important to present the actual wording of the text. Whether in these quotations one should follow the same conventions – over extending abbreviations and the like – as would be followed in a full text is a matter for careful consideration. It may well, for instance, seem over-elaborate to use italics in extending abbreviations; but creating a separate set of conventions for quotations in calendars may itself be over-elaborate in a different way.

Particular problems arise in a calendar – or, indeed, a full translation – of documents in Latin. Where a word or phrase in the original is of unusual form, or of ambiguous or uncertain meaning, it is sensible and proper to give the Latin in brackets. But great care is needed to ensure that if a word is treated this way once it is treated the same way every time it occurs; if the calendar – or translation – on mentioning a house shows that the original word was the unusual *aediculus*, the reader will reasonably assume that where a house is mentioned without the Latin being given it will be the more normal *domus*. Beyond this, often the word or phrase will be in a form that does not correspond to the syntax of the calendar, or even of the translation – a noun, for instance, may appear there as the subject of a verb but be in an oblique case in the original. To quote the original exactly at best looks odd and at worst can be misleading – it might be assumed, for instance, that an ablative form shown was actually a nominative. It can be useful here to distinguish between what

26   PthRS, 5, pp.162–70
27   PthRS, 6.

is put in quotation marks, which must exactly follow the document, and what is put in italics, which is an editorial intervention – the typographical devices used may of course differ. This way a noun can be given in the nominative, or a verb in the infinitive, without implying that it is in this form that they appear in the manuscript.

There is no reason why an edition should not be a mixture of full text and calendar, as long as it is crystal clear which is which. There can easily be coherent groups of documents – or, indeed, different parts of a single text – of which some call for fuller treatment than others. In this case, of course, there is an especially strong case for following the same conventions for the quoted passages in the calendar as for the full text. Calendaring is a device that can be used not just for reducing the length or increasing the accessibility of a text. It can also be used for documents that appear in the manuscript in some more or less intractable form: tables, elaborately bracketed lists and the like, giving their content, while changing their layout to what can be easily set out on the printed page. The whole point of a calendar is that it gives the important information – what the editor judges to be the important information – serving as a guide to the manuscript for anyone who wants to take matters further.

Calendaring is an art – though I hesitate to say so, since this might seem to encourage the inconsistency, the editorial whim, the personal quirk, that find no place in good practice. More safely we can say that it demands the same carefully controlled craftsmanship that should underlie all editing of historical texts. It is the same mixture of art and craftsmanship that is called for by the presentation of the edition on the printed page.

4

The visual presentation

Presentation and layout

The value of good presentation on the printed page can hardly be overestimated. It can do more than anything else to make the text user-friendly, easily accessible to the reader, giving differing weight to headings, text and apparatus. It can even be used, extending the metaphor we have already drawn on, to bring out the flavour of the original document. But in any case there should be no need to justify good design and good printing: any book should be visually as pleasing as possible. Many editions of records have been beautifully produced; those printed by the Roxburghe Club, such as the Elton manorial records or the correspondence relating to the restoration of the Beauchamp Chapel at Warwick, are an obvious example,[1] another is the edition of *Sir Christopher Hatton's Book of Seals* by L.C. Loyd and D.M. Stenton,[2] and the early volumes of the Dugdale Society are yet another. Others – more often in the past than now – have all too obviously been entrusted to the printer whose estimate, the lowest tendered, made no allowance whatever for time spent on planning the appearance of the page or of the book. If, of course, the finances of the publishing body are in so rocky a state that the only alternative is not to publish at all, then presumably there can be no help for it – but I suspect that this has really hardly ever been the case. Good design need not be expensive to achieve. Subscribers to the volume, far from resenting added cost, might well feel they are getting better value for their money, and given that editors will have given an enormous amount of time and expertise free of charge in preparing the text, the least the publisher can do is to produce the results of their work as attractively as possible. But whereas good design will enhance the merits of a good edition it cannot correct the imperfections of a bad one – indeed, it may well make them all the more obvious. Good design is no substitute for good editing.

1   *Elton Manorial Records 1279–1351*, ed. S.C. Ratcliff (1946); *The Restoration of the Beauchamp Chapel at St. Mary's Collegiate Church, Warwick, 1674–1742*, ed. W. Dugdale (1956).
2   *Sir Christopher Hatton's Book of Seals*, ed. L.C. Loyd and D.M. Stenton (Oxford, 1950).

I described in chapter 1 how the editorial board at Portsmouth recognised from the start the value of good presentation. Stanley Kerry, first technical adviser to the series, produced an outstanding design for the initial volume, a calendar of the borough sessions papers, 1653–88, a design that was meant to be flexible enough to serve for any sort of text, treated in any way: full text, calendar, bibliography, whatever. It has succeeded superbly: he and his successors have easily adapted it for full texts, including Latin with facing translation, a variety of calendars and a catalogue of maps. Layout and typography within the framework of the basic design are seen as a crucial aspect of each volume; they are settled, well before the book finally goes to press, on the basis of specimen printed pages, sometimes set in alternative ways, which are considered with great care by the volume's editor and the general editor, as well as by the technical adviser. The framework of the design, common to all volumes, is only one aspect of the uniform presentation throughout the series to which we attach great importance. There will be more to say of this in looking at what accompanies the text in each volume and, especially, in indexing; but the books' layout and design are the most visible aspect of this uniformity and play an important part in giving the series style, coherence and character.

Portsmouth's is of course far from being the only series of record texts to maintain a uniform – and good – typographical design and layout; the Wiltshire Record Society and the London Record Society come at once to mind, but there are many others. In one feature, however, Portsmouth is unusual. Fellow general editors and others have commented to me on the coffee-table appearance of the volumes, the air of spaciousness, with many blank areas on most pages, which they see as a great waste of paper, an extravagance beyond the reach of most record publishers. This is not quite the case. Because the page is well designed, because there is a lot of blank space, a smaller size of type can be used than would otherwise be possible – if necessary a very small type-size indeed.[3] We get as much text on the paper as many other publishers of record texts, but the blank areas – in the margins, between entries and so on – focus attention on the text and its divisions, making for easier, more efficient access.

Much of this effect is made possible by using a large page-size, A4 (297 x 210 mm). When the series was first planned I argued against this. A smaller page is nowadays more usual for record texts: many lie between 230 x 140 mm and 250 x 155 mm, and in some, like the Camden Series and the Surtees Society, it is still smaller. I thought it would be better to choose a page-size within this normal range, as it would facilitate joint publication with other record series – those for neighbouring areas, or relevant thematic series. I have never regretted that I was overruled. The advantages of the larger page-size are immense. It makes the layout of lists, tables and correspondence

3   PthRS, 6, pp.24–5.

easier and more effective; though we normally keep a wide margin for headings this can be brought into play if necessary, so that we can use the full width for complex tables. For every kind of illustration, but especially maps and reproductions of documents, the gain is obvious. It seems surprising that large format has not found more favour among record publishers since the end of the Record Commission's folio and quarto series in the 1840s. It has been used for individual publications, such as the later editions of *The Record of the Royal Society* or R.B. Patterson's edition of the charters of the first earls of Gloucester,[4] but for very few regular series of record texts. The Worcestershire Historical Society maintained for seventy years a large and handsome format (278 x 215 mm), but changed to a smaller and more conventional size in 1966; in the 1980s the Dugdale Society published two volumes in A4, but by adopting a double-column layout failed to put to full use its advantages of flexibility and appearance and abandoned the experiment. Mostly we see only the occasional large-format volume to meet the demands of a particular edition – such as the Devon and Cornwall Record Society's editions of the county maps of Benjamin Donn and Joel Gascoyne[5] – to the confusion of librarians and others who have to fit the volume on the same shelf as the rest of a series.

The principles

An edition is not a facsimile, so how far should it follow the layout of the original document? In printing a letter of a conventional form, should the sender's address and the date be set out in several lines at the top on the right, the salutation have a line to itself, the valediction and signature be placed in the centre, the addressee's name below on the left? Arguably it is better to ignore their positions on the manuscript, setting the sender's address full out on the left, running its lines together, with a note '(*top right*)', and similarly with the valediction; this certainly saves space and means there is no risk that the reader will see the page as closer to a facsimile than it really is. The magnificent edition of Charles Darwin's correspondence by Frederick Burkhardt and others, while placing the address and valediction in position on the page, runs their lines together, marking their lineation with vertical strokes.[6] Most editors, however, have fought shy of so prosaic an approach and reproduce the layout of the manuscript in full. This does something to convey the flavour of the original; moreover, information about the position of the sender's address and so on

4   *The Record of the Royal Society of London* (Royal Society; 3rd edn, 1912; 4th edn, 1940); *Earldom of Gloucester Charters*, ed. R.B. Patterson (Oxford, 1973).

5   B. Donn, *A Map of the County of Devon 1765*, ed. W.L.D. Ravenhill (new series 9; 1965); J. Gascoyne, *A Map of the County of Cornwall 1699*, ed. W.L.D. Ravenhill and O.J. Padel (new series 34; 1991).

6   *The Correspondence of Charles Darwin*, ed. F. Burkhardt et al. (Cambridge, in progress, 1985–). The note on editorial policy prefixed to each volume well repays careful attention.

leaps to the eye, and any variation from one letter – or other document – to another is immediately obvious. A sensible method is to start on a new line of print any line of text that does not run on from the previous line on the manuscript, placing the start of the line broadly where it begins on the manuscript page – left, centre or right, above or below – without attempting precise positioning. This retains the paragraphs of the original and, whether or not this is done on the manuscript, the start of a new paragraph is indented. Where the manuscript does not indent paragraphs it can be difficult to tell, where a sentence ends at the end of a line, whether a new paragraph is begun or not. This is a reminder that what we are doing is normalising the document in transferring it to print; and normalising its layout is as significant a step, to be considered just as carefully and embarked on just as cautiously, as normalising the text itself.

Normalisation of the layout can be reduced to the minimum, just like normalisation of the text. Abraham Farley's edition of Domesday Book follows the manuscripts exactly, page by page, and line by line, with every interlineation, inserted passage and marginal note precisely placed – a feat made possible by the folio format of the published book. Given that it is also printed in record type, it is as close to a facsimile as could possibly be achieved in typography. That the edition has stood the test of time so well may owe something to this: Domesday Book is a text in which great importance attaches at many points to the exact position of wording on the page.[7] But without going to this extreme, some editors either retain the lineation of the manuscript or use a vertical stroke to mark the end of each line of the original text. Retaining or indicating the lines of writing in the document avoids two small but perceptible difficulties. If, as in most editions, the lineation is normalised, a word broken with a hyphen for want of space at the end of a line is printed unbroken without the hyphen – 'bro-lken' in the manuscript appears as 'broken'. If, however, the word is one that the writer spells with a hyphen at that point, the hyphen is naturally retained: 'Lieutenant-lColonel' becomes 'Lieutenant-Colonel'. But if the word might at the time of the record be spelled with or without hyphen, and it either does not appear elsewhere in the text or else appears in both forms, the editor can only guess what to do: does 'land-lwaiter' become 'land-waiter' or 'landwaiter'? Again, if the lineation is normalised but the punctuation is not, what is to be done where there is no full stop at the end of a sentence because the writer has come to the end of a line on the page? If the edition retains or indicates the lineation, these difficulties are avoided: any ambiguity is there for the reader to see.

Reproducing tables or complicated lists from the documents can pose great problems. It is not unreasonable to admit defeat, and normalise the layout to whatever form can conveniently be accommodated – or, indeed, as we have seen, evade

7 *Domesday Book, seu liber censualis*, [ed. A. Farley] (2v., 1783).

the problem altogether and resort to calendaring, even if for these items alone. As always, so long as it is made clear that this has been done there can be no possible objection. But if it is decided to follow the form of the manuscript in printing the table, small, even very small, type can help a lot, and is certainly better than an over-crowded page: there will nearly always be many blank spaces in the table, which make it easier to read the smaller print. This device was introduced in the second volume in the Portsmouth series, an early eighteenth-century turnpike commission-ers' minute book which included their annual accounts; but our hardest test came in the dockyard papers for 1774–83, above all in a specimen of the weekly progress reports sent, on printed pro forma, from the local officials to the Navy Board, listing the ships in the dockyard, the work done on each and the number of men employed.[8] The conventions worked out then stood us in good stead in later volumes which included only slightly less complex lists and tables; some are worth mentioning here. The ruled lines, often used on the manuscript to set out the table, are omitted in the printed text, where neat columns and rows can be secured without their help and where the rulings make a heavy, ugly page; but the rulings above or below totals are retained, double or single as on the document. A long line running from an item in one column to the relevant item in the next is shown as a single en-dash, and if a series of dashes or stops serves the same purpose only the first is shown. If separate items in a column are bracketed together, they are similarly bracketed in print – some ingenuity may be needed to keep the bracketed items on a single page. However, if a single item in a column, with a word or two written on each of several successive lines, has a bracket in the manuscript to show that it is all a single item, this bracket is omitted, on the grounds that it is an aspect of lineation, normalised in editing.

In looking at these details of setting out lists and tables we may seem to have moved a long way from the general strategy of editing texts; but they serve to illus-trate how this strategy can affect minute details of typography. The typography should in fact be thought out with great care by editor and designer working togeth-er; if conventions are to be uniform in all volumes of a series – and it is to everyone's advantage, not least the readers', if they are – how they will work in a great variety of cases and contexts has to be foreseen at the start. We decided at Portsmouth that italic would be used in all circumstances to indicate the hand of the editor: explana-tory wording in the text, or any part of the text that is a stage further from the origi-nal document than the rest. Thus, in a full edition any calendared passage is in italics, and in a calendar any section that is summarised in abridged form, as well as the more obvious editorial interventions to mark a new page of the document, a marginal note, headings within the entries of a calendar or catalogue and the like. By

8   PthRS, 6, pp.24–5.

and large this has worked well and consistently; thus in a calendar or translation of a Latin text italics can properly be used to show that any words cited from the original have been normalised to a nominative or infinitive form, distinguishing this from the direct quotation in quotation marks. However, we did not foresee all the implications of this general rule for using italics. We realised only later that it meant we could not, in a full text, use italics for words underlined on the document or, in a calendar, follow the normal convention of putting ships' names in italics or – and luckily their use here is less fashionable than it was – foreign words taken over into English, such as *nisi prius* or *carte blanche*. And when it came to our calendar of adult-education records, which includes in the text quite a number of titles of printed books recommended for particular courses and so on, we had to accept that there was no practicable alternative to putting these in italics in the usual way, making an exception to our general rule.[9]

'A foolish consistency is the hobgoblin of little minds ... ,' wrote Ralph Waldo Emerson; 'With consistency a great soul has simply nothing to do'.[10] He did not have editing historical documents in mind, but even if he had it would ill become us, editors and general editors, to indulge ideas above our intellectual or spiritual station. Whether or not one aims at total consistency within a series, consistency within a single volume is of great importance. No one will be misled by our making printed-book titles an exception to our rule in using italics; practically no one will notice this, or any other tiny inconsistency in editing documents, whether in the layout or in the text – in indenting text, in the placing of full stops, in the treatment of abbreviated words or a thousand other details. Practically no one will notice if one of the violins plays a false note in a classical symphony. But unconsciously every listener, every reader, is aware of the excellence of precise playing, of consistent editing. It is a key element of that pernicketiness that lies at the heart of good editing as it lies at the heart of good typography.

The details

Achieving consistency and a pleasing printed page can both be seen as having the same end in view: making the text as easily accessible to the reader as possible. Both play a part in deciding how to show deletions, insertions and other alterations to the text of the document. If there are a great many of them, and especially if it is important to bring them to the reader's attention, a system of symbols can be used. In the manorial accounts from Cuxham the alterations made on audit were a significant feature of the edition: ⟨ ⟩ were placed round passages cancelled in any way,

9   PthRS, 5, pp.1, 19, etc.
10   R.W. Emerson, *Essays* (Boston, 1841), essay on 'Self-reliance'.

⌐ ⌐ round passages added in the same hand as the surrounding text, ⊓ ⊓ round passages in a different hand, which would usually be the hand of an auditor or the auditor's clerk. This makes these alterations easy to spot on the page, but in places gives the text a broken-up appearance, even though in the font used these symbols are neat and unobtrusive. A greater disadvantage is that the reader has to learn and remember what the symbols mean – easy enough for a spell of concentrated work on a single text, but for casual reference the notes at the front have to be consulted every time, and if the reader is using other texts as well, where the same symbols may have other meanings, they can be thoroughly confusing. In successive volumes of the Corpus of British Medieval Library Catalogues a system of uniform symbols has been developed to show the changes in these often much altered texts; it is logical and thorough and could well be widely adopted as a norm – but, unavoidably, it is complicated.[11]

These difficulties can be avoided by simply using footnotes, which have the advantage of greater flexibility and clarity. However well one has learned the symbols, 'vj ⊓j⊓ s. ⌐ <vj d.> ⌐' takes a moment or so to work out;[12] a footnote, explaining that 6 s. has been altered successively to 6 s. 6 d. by the original writer, then to 7 s. by someone else, is immediately clear. There is also the advantage that footnotes are the most elegant way of achieving uniformity within a series; of course the same symbols can be used for every text – to use different ones is to create mayhem, though this has not deterred some series of record publications – but in some texts there will be so few alterations that they will have to be shown by footnotes, as to introduce symbols to mark them would be absurd. But if footnotes are always used, there are two points to remember. One is that the passage covered by a footnote has somehow to be shown: does 'Inserted in space left blank' apply just to the word immediately before the footnote cue, or to the whole phrase, or the whole sentence? One way is to repeat the passage in the footnote, if necessary in abridged form: '"John Knight ... innholder" inserted in space left blank'. But this is clumsy, and so too is the device of placing the footnote cue at both the start and the end of the passage. A neat symbol to mark the passage in the text has the advantage of at once alerting the reader that the passage is peculiar in some way. At Portsmouth we chose half square brackets, ⌐ ⌐ , probably the least obtrusive symbol available – oddly, they are less of a visual intrusion than the symbols, ` ´ , that are sometimes used. The other point to remember in using footnotes is that they must achieve total consistency and precision. To put 'Deleted' for one word struck out, 'Struck out' for another, or to treat 'Interlineated' and 'Inserted' as two ways of saying the same

---

11   The system reached its present form in vol.4: *English Benedictine Libraries: the Shorter Catalogues*,
      ed. R. Sharpe et al. (London, 1996), pp.xiv–xv. I am grateful to Dr A.I. Doyle for telling me of it.
12   *Man.Rec.Cux.*, p.471.

thing, is to create confusion. For the Portsmouth series I maintain a long, and growing, list of the wording used in textual footnotes and use a new form only if there is no precedent for what appears on the document. Although footnotes have so far worked well in the Portsmouth series, there have been no texts where the alterations have been so many, or so important to an understanding of the document, as in the Cuxham manorial accounts. This leads to further issues.

Let us assume, following the principles set out in chapter 2, that in a full edition every alteration to the text, however minute, will be noted; however insignificant it appears to the editor, it may well have significance to some future reader of the text. This raises the interesting question of what goes in the text, what in the footnotes. Where a word in the document has been misspelled through an obvious slip of the pen the normal modern practice is to give the corrected spelling in the text, the manuscript's reading in a footnote. As Joseph Hunter put it in 1840, noting that in adopting this practice he was reversing that of Thomas Hearne a century earlier, 'This appears to be the proper way to reconcile the jarring principles, a regard to the convenience and pleasure of the reader, and a maintenance of a due reverence for the actual text'.[13] This has logical consequences for the treatment of running corrections in the text: if a word is written by mistake and immediately crossed out it will be noted only in a footnote, if a word is accidentally omitted and inserted by the writer it will be included in the text with a note that it has been added. The text is what we believe the writer meant to write. But what if a passage has apparently been deleted at a later stage, perhaps by someone other than the writer? Presumably this should be included in the text with a note of its deletion. What if, as in the Cuxham manorial accounts, the normal administrative use of the document involved successive stages of alterations and additions? Should the text be that of the first stage (with all alterations entered in footnotes) or of the last stage (noting how it has been altered since first written)? Or – as in the Cuxham records, I think rightly – should the entire text be there, including all passages deleted or added, simply showing, by symbol or footnote, the status of each? There can be no rule here. Each case must be thought through carefully, bearing in mind the reconciliation of Joseph Hunter's 'jarring principles' and remembering that an aesthetically pleasing page contributes to 'the convenience and pleasure of the reader'.

Three other details of presentation are worth mentioning. One is simplicity itself: where a document is copied within another document it can be helpful to the reader to indent it from the left-hand margin throughout, thus immediately distinguishing it from the surrounding text. The second is by way of warning against a potential trap. Two symbols widely recognised in editing texts are square brackets for words or letters supplied by the editor, nowadays normally and sensibly confined to

13   *Ecclesiastical Documents*, ed. J. Hunter (Camden Society, old series 8; 1840), p.7.

passages lost or illegible on the manuscript, not for extending abbreviations, and the series of full stops marking an omission, usually three but sometimes increased to five or more to show that the passage omitted is a long one. Where a passage is lost or illegible in the manuscript and the editor is unable to reconstruct it in square brackets, logic, not always followed here, demands that the consequent series of full stops should themselves be placed in square brackets – logic, and caution too, if one is constructing conventions for more than a single volume, for one may find oneself editing a document that, copied from another, itself uses series of stops to mark passages illegible or deliberately omitted in copying. This arose at Portsmouth in the text of the early borough customs, known only from a damaged eighteenth-century copy of a lost sixteenth-century document: there were words which the copyist could not read on the original, and others now illegible on the copy. Using a simple series of stops for the former, in this exactly following the manuscript, and a series of stops in square brackets for the latter, following here the normal usage of the series, there is no difficulty in distinguishing between the successive difficulties of the copyist and of the editor.[14]

The third detail to be mentioned is more of a problem: if the documents include printed pro formas, completed in manuscript, or letters on writing paper printed with the sender's address, how should the printed wording be distinguished? The only time this has arisen in a fully edited text at Portsmouth, a printed form for a report, we adopted an ad hoc solution – a note that all the headings were printed – which is inelegant and could not be used for a form where there were many printed passages, few manuscript additions.[15] One possibility is to use bold type for the wording in print, which has the advantage of reflecting on the printed page something of the visual relationship between the print and the manuscript of the original – flavour is brought out. But though acceptable for, say, a letterhead, bold type for a lengthily worded printed form produces a heavy and ugly page; too much bold type is overpowering, though it is of course excellent for headings and titles. A possible alternative is to underline in the printed text those passages printed in the document, but this is scarcely less obtrusive than bold type and does not reflect so well the relationship between print and manuscript in the original. It is a problem that arises in relatively few volumes of documents – many editors, many series, may never meet it, even in very modern texts – but when it does arise it is oddly intractable. We urgently need a solution at Portsmouth, for we are about to meet it head on in a number of the fully edited documents in Dr C.I. Hamilton's calendar of the dockyard papers from 1852 to 1869. A light form of bold type is likely to be the answer.

14   PthRS, 9, pp.98–103.
15   PthRS, 6, pp.23–6.

External presentation

Presentation is more than just the page of print. It is the book as a whole, including all its external features. Here, record publishing bodies mostly do justice to all the work that their editors put into their volumes. Nearly all record publications are printed on good quality paper, sewn in gatherings, and hard bound. A few societies have a long-standing tradition of paperback publication, among them the Devon and Cornwall Record Society and the Oxfordshire Record Society. A few have changed from hardback to paperback, such as the Southampton Records Series. If I were responsible for the administration of a series of record publications I should think long and hard before making this particular change. Of course there is a saving of money – but not a great deal, and because of the way hardback and paperback versions of commercially published books are costed, to produce a differential much greater than the small difference in production costs, the subscribers and other purchasers of the paperback volumes of records may well suppose they are getting less value for their money than if they were sold the same book, a little more expensively, in hardback.

I would go further. Are other features that go to make an attractive book – illustrations, a dust-jacket, even illustrated endpapers – really an extravagance in record publication? Traditionally, local record societies have operated on a shoestring, and it is immensely to their credit that such high standards of production have been maintained. The price of volumes is often absurdly low. To the four societies to which I belong I pay annual subscriptions of £15, £15, £12 and £9. Certainly they do not all publish a volume every year, but the cost is as nothing compared with the £40, £60 or £75 that one might pay for an historical monograph of the same size. Yet these same monographs, which may be less interesting, less readable, and which may very well have a shorter life, intellectually, than record texts, are published commercially and sell at a profit.

It was once explained to me by the publisher of a book I was concerned in that by spending a little extra on its external presentation, and charging a far higher sale price, more copies would be sold than by keeping the price as low as possible: purchasers like to feel they are getting an attractive, important, even an expensive, book. I do not suggest that record publishing bodies should go all the way along this path, but they might reasonably be a little less timid in investing in the outward appearance of the books they publish. There are some signs that this is happening – perhaps the Portsmouth Record Series has contributed its mite. I think, for instance, of the Royal Historical Society, which has just begun to provide its Camden Series volumes with well-designed illustrated dust-jackets. I think too of two recent editions of maps, both beautifully produced: Joel Gascoyne's map of Cornwall, published by the Devon and Cornwall Record Society in 1991, and the map of Sherwood

Forest by Richard Bankes, published by the Thoroton Society in 1997. In both cases the society could reasonably hope for significant sales outside its normal circle of members. It is a pity that the Historical Manuscripts Commission's series of joint publications had to be discontinued. Between 1962 and 1980 it published twenty-seven volumes of records, chosen for their national importance from texts submitted by local and other record societies; they were prepared for press by the Commission, designed and printed by Her Majesty's Stationery Office and published jointly with the society concerned, which paid only the run-on cost of copies for its own members. The series demanded high standards of editing, and itself contributed high standards of presentation. It probably did much to encourage improvement in both.

It is no part of my brief to consider the marketing of the published volumes; unfortunately it sometimes seems as if many record societies see it as no part of their brief either. Most British historians will have had the experience of triumphantly buying a much-needed record publication second-hand – only to discover months later that new copies could still be bought at a fraction of the price from the society that published it.[16] It is much easier to print and publish books than to sell them and this underlies much of what I have said in the last paragraph. Selling the finished product calls for good presentation, a well designed book; it also calls for effort and enterprise. Twenty years ago Dr Philip Riden persuaded the British Records Association to collaborate in an imaginative and sensible scheme to circulate widely a combined catalogue of record society publications in print, showing what could be bought, where and for how much; it did not succeed, largely because not many societies were prepared to pay the modest sum per entry needed to cover the costs.[17] However, the Internet now offers new, even cheaper opportunities of this kind, and we can only hope they will be fully explored and exploited.

This book is concerned a lot with the scholarship of editing, a little with the aesthetics of book design and not at all with the economics of marketing. All the same, I cannot help remarking that all three call for great professionalism, often achieved in the editing, sometimes achieved in the design, but seldom achieved in the marketing. This is a pity.

16   After having written this I came across a neat example: a bookseller's catalogue that offered a second-hand, 'slightly marked', copy of *The Northumberland Lay Subsidy Roll of 1296*, ed. C.M. Fraser (Society of Antiquaries of Newcastle upon Tyne, 1968), for £56. New copies of the book are still available from the Society for £5 plus postage.

17   [P. Riden], *Record Publications on Sale* (BRA, [1980]).

5

The intellectual presentation

The archival setting

It is time to advance to the third and last rule of editing:

Give full references to the documents and describe them.

Certainly the first half of this rule is usually observed – but not always. The edited text of the fifteenth-century cartulary of the Fort family of Carmarthenshire says that the manuscript is in the Public Record Office but, although a scrupulously careful edition, with an admirable analysis of the manuscript's structure and history, it gives no further reference: in fact it is among the records of the Exchequer.[1] The Camden Series edition of the minutes of the Rainbow Circle, 1894–1924, reveals their location only obliquely in the preface, in an acknowledgment to the archivist of the British Library of Political and Economic Science, 'where the Minutes are deposited', and does not give their reference there at all.[2] These, however, are exceptional cases.[3]

It is not only conventional and courteous, it is also convenient to everyone to follow the exact form of reference favoured by the particular repository, for instance placing 'MS.' before the collection name for the Bodleian Library, but for the British Library after. Real care is needed to avoid the traps set by many institutions in their systems of reference. Many references to documents in the British Library are ambiguous unless they specify whether a manuscript, that is a bound volume, or a charter, an individual document, is in question – 'MS.' or 'Ch.' The temptation to abridge apparently repetitious references starting 'Bodleian Library, MS. Bodley' or

---

1   PRO, E 163/9/39; R.A. Griffiths, 'The cartulary and muniments of the Fort family of Llanstephan', *Bulletin of the Board of Celtic Studies*, 24 (1970–2), pp.311–84. I am grateful to Mr W.R.B. Robinson for telling me of this edition.

2   *Minutes of the Rainbow Circle*, ed. M. Freeden (Camden 4th Series, 38; 1989), p.vii.

3   I am not good at finding things. However, if it turns out that, somewhere, one or both of these editions does in fact give a full reference to the manuscript I am unrepentant: it ought to be so obvious that even I cannot fail to see it.

'Public Record Office, PRO' must be firmly resisted: the Bodley manuscripts, the PRO group of records, are categories within these institutions. Only a few days before writing this I all but caused confusion by mistakenly assuming that 'Ch' in referring to a document at Corpus Christi College, Oxford, must mean 'Charter', whereas in fact it is simply an alphabetic reference – the moral of which is, always cite the reference exactly as supplied by the owner or repository.

It is, of course, not a question of giving the reference once at the start of the edition. Even if it is an edition of a single manuscript, the successive pages of a volume, membranes of a roll, have to be noted at the appropriate points in the text. Here again, care is needed to guard against traps. In the Public Record Office the numbers given to the membranes of a roll sometimes seem ambiguous to the reader: when the number is placed where one membrane is sewn to the next, which membrane does it refer to? In any repository, the older bound manuscripts often have more than one set of folio numbers, entered at various times over the centuries as leaves were added to volumes, or removed, or recombined, or simply renumbered in different ways; in the British Library the operative, current folio numbers are in pencil, often the most inconspicuous of all – yet it is these that are used for references and for ordering photocopies. And it is this, of course, that is the whole point of giving the reference. The reader must be able, without any difficulty, to refer back to the original manuscript from any point in the text or to order photocopies from the repository. The editor has a duty to the reader to ensure that the references given are adequate for this – and are correct.

It is a duty that is nearly always fulfilled. But when we come to the second half of our rule, describing the documents that are edited, it is much easier to find editions that fall short of the ideal. What is this ideal? – many editions achieve it effortlessly, because it is so natural a part of presenting a manuscript record to the world in print. At the very least the reader can properly expect to be given some idea of what the document looks like – its shape and size, whether it is paper or parchment. But there is more technical information to be given. If it is paper, the watermark should be described, with a reference to the design that most closely resembles it in Briquet, Churchill or other standard work.[4] If it is a roll, the number of membranes and how they are joined, whether Exchequer fashion, all fastened together at the top of each, or Chancery fashion, sewn end to end. If it is a book, the number of pages and the collation, how the leaves are made up in gatherings and whether any leaves have been added or removed. Again, if it is a book there should be a description of the binding. Whatever the form of the record, there should be as full an account as possible, using whatever evidence is at hand, internal or external, of how it was written:

---

4   C.M. Briquet, *Les filigranes*, ed. A. Stevenson (Amsterdam, 4v., 1968); W.A. Churchill, *Watermarks in Paper in Holland, England, France, etc.* (Amsterdam, 1935).

all at once or in successive stages, as a direct composition or copied from drafts, and so on. The various hands at work should be distinguished and the contribution of each identified. Any marginal notes, other annotations and endorsements, which will presumably be entered at the appropriate points in the text, should be described, along with any other notes or headings on flyleaves or binding or on the outer cover of a roll: who wrote all these, when and why? An important part of the description is the provenance and history of the record: who were its former owners, how did it come to be in its present location?

The editor may well come up against problems in giving this information, answering these questions – but it is the editor's job to try to solve them. Basically, archival description is not difficult, and editors are sometimes unnecessarily shy about attempting it – and in any case they can easily call in outside help. Not all the information need be given in every case; it can reasonably be assumed, for instance, that a twentieth-century letter will be written on paper, a twelfth-century charter on parchment, while there may be little to be said of a document's provenance if it remains in the archives of the administration that created it. But if in doubt it is always better to give a fuller rather than a shorter description. It is an essential part of any edition of historical records. We have seen how in printing a record one unavoidably loses something of the information provided by the original; at the very least, the full description significantly reduces this loss. But there is more to it than this. Without it, the editor is in effect inviting us to view the record *in vacuo*, divorced from its physical context, not a record source so much as an information retrieval service. This takes us a long way towards forgetting altogether that a record source is what it is and that to understand and use properly the information it provides we must understand what purpose it was intended to serve, how it was written – for how it was written will nearly always have considerable bearing on why.

In some records it is very clear that knowledge of the physical appearance of the document and of how it was put together is basic to our understanding of its contents. We have already seen how crucially important it is to distinguish the different hands at work in many manorial accounts. We see this again in, for instance, the so-called terrier of 1454 from Southampton, a survey of the properties in the town, naming their owners and identifying the section of the town wall that each had to maintain. The surviving document is a fair copy by a single, anonymous writer; his hand's other appearances in the city's archives, in records of 1446–57, suggest that it was written not long after the date of the survey given in its heading, 15 May 1454. So much is straightforward, but the later annotations and alterations, made by some ten writers in all, are more complicated. Two of them entered the names of the later owners of six properties, demonstrably in the late 1480s. Four others went through the survey systematically, adding a later name against most of the entries. The first advanced about a quarter of the way through the survey, entering names from a list of about 1500, then, perhaps discovering this list was out of date, he revised the names from another list of, probably, 1511–12; two further hands added the names from this later list to the rest of the survey and the fourth hand then checked and, where necessary, corrected the other three writers' work.[5]

In a case like this it is obvious that full understanding of the information the record gives us depends entirely on a detailed description of the manuscript that includes a close analysis of these annotators' work. In other cases, especially more modern records, the importance of describing the manuscript is less obvious. Let us look again at the Camden Series edition of the Rainbow Circle's minutes from 1894 to 1924. The Rainbow Circle was named after the Rainbow Tavern in Fleet Street, where it first met. It was, as the editor tells us, 'one of the most remarkable discussion groups of modern times in Britain. ... incorporating some of the most influential and original social and political thinkers and activists from the liberal and moderate socialist camps, it served as a testing ground and melting pot for their ideologies and policies.'[6] Their minutes are fascinating – revealing and readable – and they have been edited meticulously and sensitively. The retention of the abbreviations and layout of the original record gives us the flavour, the feel, of the original manuscripts. But this is as far as we can get. As we have seen, the manuscripts' location is revealed only incidentally, and all we are otherwise told of them is a passing reference to 'the preservation of four out of five of the Circle's minute books – the first in Ramsay MacDonald's handsomely rounded script, the fifth unfortunately vanished when a second world war German bomb destroyed the house at Gordon Square', the house, that is, where the Circle met from 1929 onwards.[7]

It is a pity we are not told more. One might suppose that a discussion group's minute books were simply its minute books, and that that was the end of the matter. In fact the most basic information about the manuscripts could add significantly to what we know of the Rainbow Circle and its workings, and of its own perception of itself. What do the minute books look like? – leather-bound from Smythson's in Bond Street with gilt lettering or hardback notebooks bought at Straker's? Did each successive secretary or minutes secretary buy a new one – this seems to be implied by the reference to MacDonald's hand in the first – or was each completely filled before starting the next? Did all the secretaries write by hand or were some minutes typewritten and pasted in? – slips of the pen in handwriting are quite different from the errors we might find in typescript. One might expect the minutes to have been written straight into the book from rough notes at the meeting; is there anything to

---

5   *The Southampton Terrier of 1454*, ed. L.A. Burgess (Southampton Records Series, 15; Historical Manuscripts Commission, Joint Publications, 21; 1976); the manuscript is described on pp.1–7.
6   *Minutes of the Rainbow Circle*, p.1.
7   *ibid.*, p.2.

show that this is how it was done? Or are there differences between one secretary and another? – this, after all, affects the quality of the record. Where were the minute books kept? Were they all together, and only one lost when the Gordon Square house was bombed, or were the rest kept separately? How did they come to be deposited in the British Library of Political and Economic Science? If they are only deposited there, not given to the Library, who owns them? All this is information that the editor must have had at his fingertips or, if not, could very easily discover. Writing it up would be a day's work at the most, and though none of these pieces of information might of itself tell us much, taken all together they would tell us a good deal – they are not just of antiquarian interest. More important still, they would turn the minute books into real, live documents, instead of simply a disembodied text.

Where is this information about the manuscript best placed? Logic might demand that it should come at the beginning of the introduction: this is what the book is all about. But it must be admitted that readers unversed in archival description might find it a rather forbidding start to the book, and if there is an historical introduction it can conveniently be placed at the end of it. This too makes sense: moving from the wider historical context we home in on the particular record. But what is so important a part of the manuscript's description that I only just fall short of calling it essential is one or more illustrations of portions of the text. A picture, obviously, can do more than any amount of description to show what the record looks like – it is not superfluous even if the original document is in typescript. But beyond this, if the record is written in a small number of hands, the illustrations can be chosen to show as many of them as possible; this can be extremely helpful to scholars working on other records where the same hands may occur – and this is as true of a twentieth-century minute book as of a thirteenth-century cartulary.

With the description of the record I would include its administrative and archival context – so closely linked with the physical description that it becomes a natural part of it, and as essential as the rest. We must know what role the record played in the organisation that created it, why it was written at all, and what other records are related to it and in what ways. Sometimes this is straightforward. Even I would grant that not much more need normally be said of the administrative role of a discussion group's minute books, though a word on any other records in the same archive could be very helpful – other records of the Rainbow Circle are mentioned only in an appendix of notes on 'some of the more interesting documents' deposited with the minute books.[8] But the administrative role – the purpose – of some records is intricate, or even if straightforward it can be difficult to elucidate. It cannot be said too

---

8   *Minutes of the Rainbow Circle*, pp.353–7; their reference in the British Library of Political and Economic Science is given, but it is not clear whether this is also the reference for the minute books themselves.

often that this is an essential part of the editor's job. One simply cannot make intelligent use of the information in the record unless we know why it was written. Without knowing this, we are moving in an area full of concealed pitfalls and other dangers impossible to guard against.

The historical setting

The historical context of the records is not essential in the way that their archival context is, but it is an important and valuable part of most editions: the contemporary background to the record, explanation and elaboration of what we are told in the text, and some assessment of the contribution its evidence can make to historical knowledge. Here the field lies open: what is offered, how much and in what form, is whatever the editor, general editor and publishing body are agreed is appropriate, whether for the particular volume or as part of wider policy. The historical context can be provided in four ways: in footnotes to the text, in the introduction, in illustrations and in appendices. I shall consider later in this chapter the role of appendices in an edition, but shall look here at each of the other three ways in turn.

Footnotes are of course invaluable for explaining particular details in the text. When I edited the short account of the Great Fire of London by Franciscus Rapicani I added some longish footnotes, the result of quite a bit of research, on the buildings on London Bridge, on the Swedish ambassadors' lodgings in Covent Garden and Westminster, on a contemporary Dutch account of the near-lynching, described in the text, of a Swedish nobleman by the mob who thought the fire was the work of foreigners, and on other matters.[9] This research helped me to understand the text more fully, and I hope the footnotes helped my readers too. Elucidatory footnotes of this kind are often especially useful in editions of, say, diaries or correspondence that are likely to command a wide non-specialist readership. In the Portsmouth series, on the other hand, we follow an austere policy of avoiding these more discursive historical notes, restricting footnote explanations to points where they are needed to understand the text. Thus when the Portsmouth garrison on 15 July 1799 celebrated 'the Recent Brilliant Victory, obtained by His Majesty's Allies in Italy' with a *feu de joie* – each soldier in the line fired his musket in turn to produce a continuous sound – it seemed reasonable to explain that this was for the battle of Trebbia, fought on 17–19 June.[10] It is a question of whatever seems right for the particular text or set of texts.

What is not appropriate for a footnote, however, is a comment or explanation

9   P.D.A. Harvey, 'A foreign visitor's account of the Great Fire, 1666', *Transactions of the London and Middlesex Archaeological Society*, 20 (1959–61), p.86–7.

10   PthRS, 7, p.58.

that applies to a number of different places in the text – unless the editor is prepared to give a cross-reference back to this footnote at every relevant point. The footnote that explains something the first time it occurs, with no explanation on subsequent occurrences, is utterly unhelpful. A published record text is usually a work of reference. Clearly this is something that differs from one text to another – many users may for instance read the whole of a volume publishing a diary or correspondence. But most record publications will be read by hardly anyone from beginning to end apart from the editor, the general editor and the more conscientious reviewers. They are books one looks things up in – names, places, subjects, whatever – not a good read, a fact that some editors find difficult to accept, having entered into a close relationship with a text they will have come to know almost by heart. It is a point I shall return to, in looking at the glossary and, above all, the index. I introduce it here only to say that the proper place for any comment or explanation that applies throughout the text is not a footnote but the introduction.

I have heard it said that it is wrong to give more than the briefest historical introduction to a record text; as it is meant as a source to be used by other historians, the editor should not exhaust its potential – something should be left for everyone else. I am unconvinced. If it is possible to exhaust the text's potential in even the lengthiest of introductions it can hardly be worth publishing at all; it should surely be capable of contributing to more than a single monograph. On the other hand I would entirely agree that we should not have an introduction that dominates the whole book, overwhelming the text itself – the tail (which in this case comes first) should not wag the dog. The text is what the book is all about, and the purpose of the introduction is to introduce the text. It is a matter not of length but of weight and focus: the introduction can be as long and as complicated as may be, provided it is concentrated on the record itself, elucidating, analysing and generally setting it in context, a context that may be drawn as a very broad picture. A good example of what I mean is the splendid edition of the two twelfth-century surveys of Winchester by Frank Barlow. The survey of c.1110 occupies 38 pages of print, the survey of 1148, 73 pages. The entire volume, however, comprises over 600 pages, much of this being taken up with a very full account of twelfth-century Winchester, from the surveys and other sources, by Professor Martin Biddle and Dr D.J. Keene. But the text is still the focus, the centre of the entire work: throughout, it is what the book is all about, and it is in no way swamped by all that accompanies it.[11]

Also in this Winchester volume is an important study, by Olof von Feilitzen, of the personal names and bynames recorded in the surveys. It seems to me wholly proper, if opportunity offers, to include with the edited text an excursus on some

---

11   *Winchester in the Early Middle Ages: an Edition and Discussion of the Winton Domesday*, ed. M. Biddle (Winchester Studies, 1; Oxford, 1976).

specialised topic, a study of what the record's evidence contributes to that field of research; it can be seen almost as a sample of the wares, the sort of thing that the record can be used for. A forthcoming Portsmouth volume, a calendar of the borough sessions papers from 1689 to 1700 by Mrs Margaret Hoad, will include a discussion by the late Jean Robertson, full of interest, on the fragments of reported speech in the papers and what they can tell us of contemporary conversation, the spoken language of the time. But one word of warning is in order here. We have seen in chapter 1 how secondary work based on the records will date much faster than the editions of the records themselves. The edited text, if not for all time, is at least for all the foreseeable future. But of the writings accompanying the text in the volume we can broadly say that the further they are from the text itself, the shorter their shelf-life will be. The archival description, the archival context, will probably date little, if at all; but the historical introduction and notes will soon begin to seem out of date, as further work is done on the subject and the frontiers of knowledge advance, and a more specialised contribution may well be superseded quickly and completely. This is something one must just accept: it is no reason to refrain from including any historical context. The record deserves to be introduced to its readers in this way, and the readers deserve the assistance that this introduction can give. Fully focused on the particular record, it is likely that it will still offer particular insights long after much of its main thrust seems out of date. We have come a long way in our knowledge and understanding of medieval manorial courts since F.W. Maitland wrote the introduction to his volume of select pleas from these records in 1889, but it is still basic reading for anyone working in this field.[12] Admittedly this was Maitland – but the same could be said of many other editors' introductions.

Certainly illustrations will not date. We have already seen pictures of the record itself as an important part of the archival context. Pictures drawn from contemporary sources are an interesting, even important, part of the historical context. They are not so much a part of the historical introduction as akin to the related texts that may be printed in appendices, and they can be immensely helpful in bringing to life what might on the surface seem a dull topic. A good example is the catalogue of poor-law records from Sussex, published in 1960, which includes pictures and a plan of eight nineteenth-century workhouses, an extraordinary variety of buildings, ranging from pleasant-looking country cottages to the grimly prison-like structures of the towns; at once one realises that these records are about real places, and about real people who lived there.[13] The calendar of Portsmouth adult-education records, 1886–1939, seemed an unpromising subject for illustrations, but photographs of three of the lecturers and a lively portrait by Elizabeth Polunin of a fourth make a

12   *Select Pleas in Manorial and other Seignorial Courts*, ed. F.W. Maitland (Selden Society, 2; 1889).
13   *Sussex Poor Law Records*, ed. J.M. Coleman (Chichester, 1960).

substantial contribution to the volume, again helping to turn the names in the text into real people.[14]

On the endpapers of this volume of adult-education records we reproduced two of the handsomely designed certificates given to the successful students in the 1890s. If one is lucky enough to be allowed pictures on the endpapers these are an opportunity for some flight of imagination, as they can be seen as purely illustrative, setting the scene for the text without the serious purpose that one might think necessary to justify the book's other pictures. On the endpapers of the Customs letter-books of 1748–50 we reproduced a tiny portion of a table from Postlethwayt's *Universal dictionary of trade and commerce* of 1757 showing the incredible complexity of the duties the officers had to collect. On 'Babies, or puppets for children, the groce, containing 12 dozen', 17s. under an act of 12 Charles II, a further 3s.5d. and 3.9 twentieths if brought in by a British importer or 3s.7d. and 17.4 twentieths if by a foreigner, of which 3s. and 2.25 twentieths would be repaid if they were re-exported; on 'Babies heads of earth, the dozen', there was a different set of rates, on 'Babies jointed, the dozen (Toys)' another, and so on.[15] If produced as a formal illustration with caption, in the introduction or text, it might seem a clumsy way of making the point, better achieved by a few lines in the introduction; on the endpapers, without caption, it tells its story unobtrusively but all the more cogently.

Our first essay in endpaper illustration was, however, unpropitious. For the borough sessions papers, 1653–88, we chose a manuscript map (not, to be honest, immediately relevant) of Portsmouth and its surrounds, which stated in its title that it was 'done in the year 1716'. Naively, I entered it in the list of illustrations as 'Survey of Portsea Island 1716' – only to discover, seven years later when we published Mr Donald Hodson's catalogue of maps, that it really dates from the mid-1740s, copied indeed from a map of 1716 and updated in a number of details but repeating the date in the title-panel unaltered.[16] There is more than one moral to be drawn from this.

Appendices

Endpapers can be fun and so too can appendices. However austerely defined the editorial strategy may be, they can in a sense lie outside it, a kind of free-text field that follows the more strictly controlled edited records, less constrained and offering more scope for editorial fancy. I speak, of course, only of the strategy: I would not suggest that any documents in appendices should be edited less carefully than the rest. But appendices can be valuable too, expanding and reinforcing all parts of the

14 PthRS, 5.
15 PthRS, 8.
16 PthRS, 4, pp.12–13.

introduction and helping to set the text in its archival and historical context. They can also be valuable in the strategy of the series as a whole, not just of the individual volumes: they can be used as a way of publishing documents too short to fill a volume and thus of eliminating the miscellany volumes that are the bane of so many record-publishing bodies. Instead of bringing together unrelated odds and ends in a volume that none but the members of the society will buy, for no would-be purchaser will be interested in more than one or two bits, they can, so to speak, share the introduction and other apparatus with the main text and are immediately at hand for readers whose interests will already have led them to the volume. Moreover, there are some documents which, though of great interest, are too slight to be published individually in a miscellany. An example is the exercise book of essays written by J.H. Matthews (he became Sir James) as a university extra-mural tutorial-class student in 1909–10, annotated by his tutor, W.T. Layton (he became Lord Layton); as an appendix to the calendar of Portsmouth adult-education records it is invaluable, an extraordinarily lucky chance survival, which, like the pictures of the tutors, puts flesh on the bare bones of the administrative documents – it at once shows what the extra-mural operation was all about.[17] If published by itself, however, it would lose most of its point.

Each volume so far published in the Portsmouth series includes from four to ten appendices. They are arranged, silently, in a fixed order (no volume contains more than a few of the categories): specimen full texts of documents in a calendar; additional documents, whether full texts or in any other form, in chronological order; lists of documents; lists of persons; any other lists or tables, ending with a table of the statutes mentioned in the volume; concordance or index of manuscripts. A brief look at the appendices published there will bring out some general points, but we shall look at them in a different order: first those so important that (whether they are called appendices or not) they are all but an essential part of the volume; then those that, though less crucial, can be seen as significant props supporting the text; and finally those that illustrate, explain or enlarge the coverage of the text – the real fun ones.

We have already seen that texts of specimen documents are a necessary part of a calendar – part of the contract with the reader that permits publication as a calendar instead of the full text. Just as necessary, where this is possible, are lists and tables giving information drawn from all of a group of documents when only a selection or a tranche has been edited: they play a key role in justifying the decision to produce a selective edition, and this is how I see the lists of ships built and of ships docked that are appended to the Portsmouth dockyard papers of 1774–83.[18] A similar unspoken

17   PthRS, 5, pp.177–94.
18   PthRS, 6, pp.158–65.

contract underlies publication of documents arranged differently from their order in the original manuscripts or archives: an index must be provided so that one can find where any individual document or page of a manuscript is entered in the printed text. This has been done at Portsmouth for the borough sessions papers, published in chronological order different from their arrangement in bundles, and for the catalogue of maps, which draws its entries from a great range of repositories and arranges them by category of map and by date.[19] For the dockyard papers of 1774–83, drawn from twenty-four volumes in the National Maritime Museum and printed in, from the archival angle, haphazard order, no index of manuscripts was supplied; given that most of the volumes have their leaves unnumbered, so that references within them have to be by the letter's date, that many documents are not fully calendared but summarised, and that many more have been drawn on for lists and tables, an index from the manuscript references would have been a daunting task – but it is something that should be considered for future dockyard-paper volumes, perhaps covering just the fully calendared documents. I would also class among these all-but-essential appendices any further documents that underlie the edited text and are necessary to a proper understanding of it. The only ones from Portsmouth that I place in this category are with the minute book of the trustees of the turnpike from Portsmouth to Sheet, 1711–54: the complete texts of the acts of 1711, 1726 and 1742 under which the trust operated.[20]

In my second category of appendices, those that are significant props supporting the text, I would place two further groups of supplementary documents. There are those which are excluded from the main text by the strict application of demarcation lines but which are so close to it that it would be unhelpful to leave them out altogether; the fifteenth-century list of now lost deeds of Sheen Priory, appended to the Portsmouth calendar of deeds, is one example, and the tracings of pre-1860 maps attached to reports of the 1860s, listed in an appendix to the catalogue of maps, is another.[21] Then there are documents that are very closely related, textually or administratively, to the edited text; with the Portsmouth royal charters, for instance, a section of the text in the warrant for the 1627 charter that was left out of the final version.[22] Also in this props-to-text category I would place the table of statutes that we have included in every Portsmouth volume that anywhere refers to specific acts of Parliament; it gives the citation and title of each, drawn from *The Statutes of the Realm*, *The Statutes at Large*, *A Collection of the Local and Personal Acts* and *The Public and General Acts*. This avoids the need to give this information in footnotes, and it

19   PthRS, 1, pp.180–3; 4, pp.151–5.
20   PthRS, 2, pp.169–78.
21   PthRS, 11; 4, pp.128–34.
22   PthRS, 9, pp.113–14.

has proved its worth on one occasion by revealing that an act of Parliament mentioned in the introduction from a secondary work simply did not exist – the mistake perhaps originated in confusion with an order in Council.

In my third category, appendices that illustrate and enlarge on the edited record, I would again place some further documents that can do much to place the text in its broader context. There are those that, while not closely linked to the text, are still related to it and can valuably supplement it – like the Portsmouth entries in the Customs register of seizures for 1748–50 which tie up with references in the edited letter-books or, in the edition of Portsmouth royal charters, the borough's request for a charter in a petition to the queen in about 1585, a petition which was unsuccessful but which may have some bearing on the charter actually granted in 1600.[23] Again, there are documents not directly related to the text but on the same topic, documents which might or might not qualify for publication by themselves in a miscellany volume but which can usefully be published here in a ready-made context which they in fact enhance. Thus Portsmouth's early borough custumal – a complex sixteenth-century document including earlier elements and known only in an eighteenth-century copy – was published with the royal charters,[24] and the appendices to the Corporation's formal record of 1731–51 included the magnificent 200-line poem, printed in 1751, on local political events, *The geese in disgrace*:

> In Days of yore, when Brutes (content
> With Nature's Laws and Government)
> Knew no Ambition, Envy, Strife,
> Or any Bane of social Life, ...
> Each knew his Duty, Rank and Place,
> The Fox "My Lord, the Wolf "Your Grace,
> The Ass, "Your Honour, and the Goose
> "Good Mr. Alderman! What News? ... [25]

A contemporary cartoon, based on the poem, contributed the volume's endpapers. Lists of people, which I would also place in this category, can take two forms. There are simple lists of office-holders, which can be far from simple to compile and which can add a lot to the volume's value as a work of reference. To the Customs letter-books of 1748–50 I added a list of all officers on the Portsmouth establishment from 1671 to 1750; producing it was an appalling job, involving a search of some 250 quarterly establishment lists, but it substantially contributes to the volume's claim to serve as a guide to the records from the 1671 re-organisation to the mid-eighteenth

23   PthRS, 8, pp.205–13; 9, p.112.
24   PthRS, 9, pp.98–103.
25   PthRS, 3, pp.79–89.

century.[26] Besides the straightforward lists of names there are prosopographical lists, series of tiny biographies. Those of the Portsmouth aldermen and burgesses of 1731–51 are a most valuable compilation, throwing much light on the personal and political implications of the edited record.[27]

My three categories of appendix are no more than a rough guide, and likewise my division between the various kinds of supplementary document that can be printed. I have not remotely exhausted the possibilities of appendices that can be added to a record text, nor of their value, the use that can be made of them in particular instances. However important some appendices are – above all the specimen full texts in a calendar, the index of manuscripts and the most closely related documents – they are not quite essential and our three rules of editing make no mention of them. But often they have a crucial role to play in the intellectual presentation of the record.

Glossary

The glossary too is part of the text's intellectual presentation. As with particular points of historical explanation, we must remember that few users of the text will read it from end to end, so a footnote explaining an unusual word only the first time it occurs will not be helpful. Recurring words and phrases that refer to the forms or procedures of the organisation that created the records are often best explained in the introduction where they can be fully discussed along with the administration itself, and this is where the reader will most naturally expect to find them. Words dealt with in this way in the Portsmouth dockyard papers of 1774–83 include *extra* (overtime), *superannuation* (retirement on pension) and *chips* (the workers' perquisite of the bits of wood that fell from the axe or adze).[28] But most words that need explaining are best defined in a glossary. If it is a Latin text for which the editor is supplying a list showing how particular abbreviated words have been extended, this can easily incorporate the glossary – in the Cuxham manorial records I distinguished the glossarial words by putting them in bold type.

How do we choose which words to put in the glossary? In a way this is easier for medieval texts, whether in Latin, French or English, than for later English ones. The specialists who use these texts will normally have access to standard dictionaries and will expect to make use of them in reading any text likely to contain unusual words. We can thus restrict the glossary to words that do not appear in the *Dictionary of Medieval Latin* or – for the second half of the alphabet, as it has reached only the

26 PthRS, 8, pp.219–24.
27 PthRS, 3, pp.94–115.
28 PthRS, 6, pp.xliii, xlvi-xlviii.

letter L – in the *Revised Medieval Latin Word-List*; or in the *Anglo-Norman Dictionary*; or in the *Middle English Dictionary*, now happily advanced nearly to the end of un-.[29] It should, however, include hitherto unrecorded spellings of known words, partly for the sake of the reader, who may fail to recognise them, and partly by way of contributing to knowledge, for the glossary serves a twofold purpose. Primarily, of course, it is an aid to the reader of the edited text, but it is likely to be drawn on by others too, not only the lexicographer who will find it invaluable to have all the text's new words and spellings drawn together in this way, but also the more numerous readers of other similar documents, in print or in manuscript, who may well turn to the edition for help on difficult words or readings they have found.

This is equally true of post-medieval English texts; and here again we can start from the assumption that any word that is not in, say, the *Shorter Oxford English Dictionary* will be put in the glossary. But beyond this the situation is more complicated. We cannot expect every reader of our text to have the dictionary at hand, and there are a fearful lot of words in the *Shorter OED* that are unfamiliar even to readers of historical records. The reader deserves more help than this. The editor of the text may well be the least qualified person to choose the words for the glossary, being a specialist in the subject of the record and thus so familiar with its vocabulary as to be unable to tell what words anyone else is unlikely to know. The general editor, unless also familiar with the subject, may well be a better judge. As a guide to drawing up the glossary for Mrs Hanna's calendar of Portsmouth-area medieval deeds I consulted a specialist in nineteenth-century local and political history, and was startled to realise what an elaborate jargon medievalists use among themselves: words such as *escheat, purpresture, tithingman*, are common currency among medieval historians, but not among the wider public for whom the book is also intended. If, as here, the edition is a calendar, in modern English, should it not be possible to avoid words that are not in normal usage? Unfortunately it is not. *Escheat, purpresture, tithingman* and many more are not simply difficult words used by specialists when a better-known word would serve just as well; they really are the only possible words for what they represent, and short of elaborate, even misleading, circumlocutions there is no alternative to using them.

The vocabulary of medieval administrative, legal and agrarian history is well covered by the *Shorter OED*. Other specialist vocabularies are less well covered, even by the full *Oxford English Dictionary*, and one may have to go further afield for

29   *Dictionary of Medieval Latin from British Sources*, ed. R.E. Latham and D.R. Howlett (London, in progress, 1975–); *Revised Medieval Latin Word-List from British and Irish Sources*, ed. R.E. Latham (London, 1965); *Anglo-Norman Dictionary*, ed. L.W. Stone and W. Rothwell (Modern Humanities Research Association; 7v., 1977–92); *Middle English Dictionary*, ed. H. Kurath et al. (Ann Arbor, in progress, 1956–).

definitions. For the Portsmouth Customs letter-books of 1748–50, Wilhelmsen's *English Textile Nomenclature*, intriguingly published in Norway in 1943, proved invaluable for, especially, the names of Indian cotton cloths, while Crouch's *Complete Guide to the Officers of His Majesty's Customs*, published in 1732, filled in some awkward gaps in the words used in certain Customs procedures.[30] Sometimes the specialist work, seeing the word in its technical context, offers a fuller or more precise definition than the *OED*. Whatever source is used to define a word it is, to say the least, good practice – I should like to say it is essential – to give the source of the definition, even if this source is as obvious as the *OED*. Glossaries for edited records abound in definitions which, to repeat R.E. Latham's words, originate in 'an erudite ingenuity that evokes admiration rather than confidence'.[31] Editors owe it to all their readers to command their confidence, and to say not only what they think the word means but also why they think so, giving references for their sources as they would for any other information. It is also sensible and helpful to give the references to the entries where each word in the glossary occurs, creating a glossarial index; the editor, after all, will have this information more or less readily to hand and there seems no reason not to pass it on to the reader.

It is good practice too to put a marker in the text every time a word appears that is in the glossary – or, if some words are often repeated, just the first time a word appears in each entry. As Dr C.I. Hamilton put it, referring to his forthcoming edition of Portsmouth dockyard papers for 1852–69, marking every instance 'might have led to an outbreak of smallpox' in entries where many words had to be marked – smallpox because the Portsmouth series puts an asterisk before each word that is in the glossary. This convention may have been a mistake; though it has not happened yet, sooner or later we shall be baffled by having to print a text that itself contains asterisks, and some more esoteric symbol would have been better.

Notes on editing

Having begun this chapter with the third rule of editing, let us end it with a further look at the second rule, 'Say what you are going to do and do it'. Saying what you are going to do is difficult only in deciding what to leave out. By the time a conscientiously edited full text or calendar is ready for the press there will have accumulated an immense number of notes on the precedents and conventions followed. Some may be common to the series as a whole, others peculiar to the volume, points that have arisen in the course of the work. To set them all out in full would call for many pages

30　L.J. Wilhelmsen, *English Textile Nomenclature* (Skrifter fra Norges Handelshøyskole, 1; 1943); H. Crouch, *A Complete Guide to the Officers of His Majesty's Customs in the Out-Ports* (London, 1732).

31　*Revised Medieval Latin Word-List*, p.ix.

of print – but of course this is not necessary. The general editor may maintain a compendium of precedent and practice in innumerable details, but it would be wrong to inflict them on the editor of an individual volume, let alone its readers.

Many series of record publications produce style sheets, to set the editor off on the right lines, a guide to some of the more obvious conventions to follow; the Hakluyt Society, for instance, produced a thirty-page printed *Guide* for its editors. I intended to do this at Portsmouth, and produced a first short draft which I supposed would gradually expand into a full guide to the conventions. That this has never happened is due not to inertia but to growing realisation that, say, Latin text with facing translation, the full text of an eighteenth-century record, a bibliography of maps and a calendar of nineteenth- and twentieth-century papers are very different propositions. The same principles may underlie them, the same conventions may govern their presentation, but any editor would find that of a set of rules covering them all some two-thirds would not apply to the particular volume. I find it easier and more practical to ask the editor as far as possible to follow the precedent of previous volumes and to produce a short specimen of the text at an early stage. We can then go through this carefully settling how the conventions of the series are to be applied in this case. Any points not fully covered then can be cleared up on copy-editing.

Which, then, of the mass of conventions and precedents within the programme do we actually put up-front? If it is a rule of editing that we say what we are going to do, what do we say? How much do we tell? A lot can be left to speak for itself. There is normally no need, for instance, to burden the reader with the rules followed in the layout of the document on the printed page, even though these rules have been carefully worked out and scrupulously observed. However, the principles governing the transcription of the text itself should certainly be set out: what is done with the long *i* and the pointed *u* of a medieval text, whether the text's punctuation and capital letters have been normalised in any respect, how abbreviations have been dealt with and which, if any, have been expanded silently. It is helpful to mention any points where the text produces ambiguities – little differentiation between full stops and commas, for instance, or difficulty in deciding whether a compound word is written as one word or two. I would not suggest that more than one or two pages of print should be given to setting out the way the text has been edited; it is the clarity of broad principles that is called for, rather than the complexity of detailed rules. The editing of the text is like the orchestration of a musical score: if it is well composed and correctly executed it will seem right and there is no need for the simple listener – the normal reader – to know a great deal about the technicalities below the surface. It is not incompatible with our second rule of editing for a good edition to exemplify the art that conceals art.

6

The index

Overall strategy

We have seen that most readers will treat most editions of historical records as works of reference. They are books to look things up in, not books to read. It follows that the index will normally be the key to the whole work and thus of crucial importance. Anything missing from the index will be all but lost from the record. Moreover, the index will be the starting point for most readers, their first impression of the book. It should be as efficient, as user-friendly, as welcoming, as it possibly can be. It should be instantly understandable, without having to read any instructions first, but notes for guidance should be readily at hand, at the start of the index, to be consulted if needed. Everything possible should be done to avoid irritating the reader – never, for instance, give a cross-reference that leads only to another cross-reference. In this, as in all else, the index sets the tone for the book as a whole.

In discussing indexing here I shall look only at a few of the issues affecting strategy; along with others they are discussed by Dr R.F. Hunnisett in his admirable *Indexing for Editors*, which also deals fully with the tactics, the nuts and bolts of indexing edited records.[1] One small practical hint I would offer at the start. Even in these days of computer indexing programs, which take so much of the sheer drudgery from the work, one still finds oneself drafting parts of the index on slips of paper or cards – entries for abstract subjects and the like. Use paper or cards already printed or written on one side, not from a zeal for economy run riot, but because it avoids a hazard that can easily lead to the loss of entries: accidentally writing two entries on a slip that is blank on both sides.

How many indexes should there be? We have already looked at the index of manuscripts that certain volumes will need and in a very few cases the editor may feel tempted to create other special indexes, of field-names, say, or names of ships. The temptation should be resisted if at all possible. In principle the fewer separate indexes there are the better. A case can be made for a separate index of subjects and I shall

---

1   R.F. Hunnisett, *Indexing for Editors* (BRA, Archives and the User, 2; 1972).

discuss it later in this chapter, but I see no case whatever for dividing persons from places in separate indexes. It is irritating to the user, who as often as not will start searching the wrong one, and it can be really unhelpful to separate, say, the entries for Berkeley Castle, Gloucestershire, from those for the Berkeley family who lived there, while anyone might wonder whether to look up 'London, Lord Mayors of' in one index or the other – are they persons or an aspect of a place?

Another question that must be settled at the start is whether to index by page number or by entry number. Indexing by entry number offers significant advantages. The entry will normally be shorter than a page, so it is easier for the reader, having got the reference from the index, to locate what is being sought, while it means that the editor can fully prepare and check the index while the work is in progress – indexing by page number can be done only when page proofs come to hand, by which point a tight schedule will be in operation, so that the work has to be done in a great hurry. On the other hand, whereas pages are of limited length, entries are not; they may well extend over more than a page, making it harder, not easier, for the reader to find the reference. One answer is to split up long entries into, if possible, less than page-length subsections – in which case avoid one subtle trap we fell into at Portsmouth. We use letters for the subsections – 12a, 12b and so on – but, extending deep into the alphabet, did not realise till too late that, since we use not aligning figures (1,2,3,4) but non-aligning ones (1,2,3,4), 12o in the index was indistinguishable from 120: 120.

But whatever is done in one volume in a series, right or wrong, stick to it throughout. Many readers will be consulting not just the one edition through the index, but several or all of the volumes in the series, one after the other. Even finding you are looking up the wrong index is less irritating than discovering that what in one volume is indexed as 'Warwick, earls of: Guy Beauchamp' appears in the next as 'Beauchamp, Guy, earl of Warwick', or that 'Neithrop, in Banbury, Oxfordshire' next becomes 'Banbury, Oxfordshire: Neithrop', or that 'gardens' are given their own heading in one volume, are a subheading of 'houses' in the next and are not indexed at all in the third. Uniform presentation enhances and adorns a series of record publications; uniform indexing, however, is essential to its efficient use. Many series achieve this uniformity: the Public Record Office calendars and the Wiltshire Record Society are two examples. Others, however, simply do not recognise its importance, and allow the editor of each volume to index it as seems best. Few readers will have thanked them.

Persons and places

The editor of one record publication I was involved in told me that as the edition was meant primarily for family historians – a perception I did not in fact share – there was no point in including forenames in the index: a reader interested in one person named Robinson would be interested in them all. I doubt if this line of reasoning would appeal to many family historians, and it was not put into effect; but there is one simplification of persons' names in the index which I favour but which some might question. Let us take abridged sequences of index entries from two outstandingly good editions of medieval records:

> Carlton
> Ralf de ...
>   Henry and Robert his sons ...
> Ralf de [probably another one] ...[2]

> Whitley
> Richard of (two of this name both d. by 1305,
>   identities uncertain) ... ; one = Richard son
>   of William of Whitley ...
> —*another*, son of Richard ...[3]

In each case (and there are others in both indexes) the editor has come up against a problem that is very common in both medieval and later records. References to a single name occur in contexts that make it likely, or certain, that there are two namesakes, while it may occur again in other contexts that offer no way of telling which of these namesakes is in question. In both these cases the editor has done the best he can to help the reader in this difficulty.

This is, of course, entirely proper; but it produces clumsy index entries, and implies that in most cases, where there is no caveat of this sort, all references under a single name refer to a single person – which often an editor cannot possibly tell. A neater and more satisfactory way of dealing with the problem is to add a footnote when it becomes clear that one has namesakes on one's hands, explaining which is which in other references where they can be distinguished and adding cross-references from these points.[4] This may seem to fly in the face of all my strictures in the last chapter against explaining words or historical details at the point where they first appear in the text – but it does not. Anyone using the index to look up Ralf de Carlton or Richard of Whitley will find this information as surely as if it was entered in the index itself, and now it will also be available for anyone who reaches the entry by some other route.

Our index will then enter all the references to Carlton, Ralf de, or to Whitley,

2   *Rufford Charters*, ed. C.J. Holdsworth (Thoroton Society, Record Series; 4v., 1972–81), iv, p.585.
3   *Reading Abbey Cartularies*, ed. B.R. Kemp (Camden 4th Series, 31, 33; 1986–7), ii, p.465.
4   Professor Kemp does just this for the Whitley family (*ibid.*, ii, p.335); the index note is an added guide.

Richard of, in a single list, without any attempt to distinguish namesakes. In other words, what we are indexing is names, not people. A corollary is that as our index does not distinguish two people with the same name, so it does not bring together references to the same person under different names. If they were all so called in the text,[5] my sequence of entries under Whitley would be:

> Whitley
>   Richard of ...
>   Richard son of Richard of ...
>   Richard son of William of ...

I do not wish to proceed further here into the quagmire of medieval personal names, partly because Dr Hunnisett explains and charts it so clearly, partly because the points I am making apply to names of all periods, not just the middle ages. But I would add this further point which applies especially to medieval names. In indexing names, not people, one can be very precise in one's entries. 'John son of William Smith' becomes 'Smith, John son of William', whereas 'John Smith son of William Smith' has separate entries for 'Smith, John' and 'Smith, William'; 'Margaret wife of William Smith' becomes 'Smith, Margaret wife of William'. This avoids any of the rationalisation that could falsify the record: unless they are actually so called in the text we should never assume that William's wife was called Margaret Smith or his son John Smith – they may have used entirely different (and unrecorded) second names.

However, when we come to persons of note, clearly identified in the record and likely to be looked for individually by users of the index, our index of names, not of persons, may seem hardly adequate. I do not really suggest that entries for the first Earl of Chatham and his second son should be lumped together in a single entry under 'Pitt, William'. There is no reason why an index where the personal entries are in principle entries of names, not people, should not include, as appropriate, entries of notable individuals, distinguished by a word of two to identify them. Successive entries thus might read:

> Pitt
>   William, *1st Earl of Chatham* ....
>   William, *statesman, d.1806* ...
>   William ...

The last entry would give the references to any other less distinguished William Pitts who appeared in the record. This mixture of entries of names and entries of persons

---

5   In point of fact, Richard son of Richard of Whitley is always simply Richard of Whitley in the printed documents.

may seem confusing; in practice it works well. One seldom, after all, has difficulty in distinguishing notabilities from their namesakes. Who is selected for this individual treatment is of course a decision for the particular index, except that there should certainly be uniformity throughout a series: the reader should not find that someone entered as an individual in one volume appears only as a name in the next. The Public Record Office's automated catalogue of seals, now in preparation, is sparing in identifying individuals: sovereigns, their consorts and children, peers and their spouses, diocesan bishops, and no one else. In the Portsmouth series we have been more prodigal, extending identifying descriptions to anyone in the *Dictionary of National Biography*, anyone of high rank in the armed forces or other government service, and officers of Portsmouth corporation. The system avoids many of the traps that beset personal-name entries in indexes of record texts.

Many more can be avoided by following the Latham-Hunnisett rules for standardising the index-entry forms of surnames – I cannot commend these rules too highly, for they at once bring order and method into an area which has suffered from much anarchy in the past. I will not rehearse the rules here – Dr Hunnisett sets them out clearly and in detail[6] – but an outline of their general principles is not out of place. They involve separate rules for each of three broadly defined periods which correspond to changing practice in surname usage and in orthography:

1   Before 1500. The name is entered under the modern English form of the occupation, the place, the topographical feature, the personal characteristic, the forename used as patronymic, or whatever other word is used as surname or byname. Thus Faber, Smythe, le Fevre, all appear under Smith; atte Welle, ad Fontem, under Well; filius Johannis under John; and so on. The forms found in the record are entered in parentheses after the form used for the heading – 'Smith (Faber, le Fevre, Smythe)' – and cross-references given from them: 'Faber, *see* Smith'.

2   1500–1750. The name is entered in its modern form but without bringing together the forms that originate in a different language, so Faber and Smith now count as different names. Otherwise the text's own forms are given in parentheses as before, and cross-references added – though rather fewer will now be needed.

3   After 1750. The name is entered in the exact form of the record, so that Smith and Smythe now count as different names. However, in cases like this – and there will probably be quite a number of them – it is helpful to give cross-references unless the variant forms are all but adjacent in the index.

I have followed these rules in the Public Record Office's catalogue of seals and (slightly

---

6   Hunnisett, *Indexing for Editors*, pp.41–4.

modified for the middle period) in the Portsmouth series and I have found that they work extremely well. In one respect they work rather better than Dr Hunnisett himself suggests. He notes of the earliest period that 'up to ten per cent of surnames in many volumes will prove unamenable to standardisation and must be indexed in their manuscript forms'.[7] In my experience this is unduly pessimistic; there will always be a hard core of names, especially those deriving from place-names, that call for quite a lot of work to identify them – to find, for instance, that it really is Turweston, not Turnstone – but most of the answers will eventually come to light. Certainly there will always be an irreducible minimum, as often as not because the writer misheard or misunderstood what he was told – there will have been no one to tell him how to spell it correctly – but I would not put this at more than two or three per cent of the names.

Dr Hunnisett, very properly, argues that the rules must be followed rigorously. Because some names are traditionally spelled in a form that does not accord with them we must not be deflected but must treat them the same way as any other. Wat Tyler thus appears under Tiler, with a heading that might well read 'Tiler (Tegularius, Tyler, le Tylere)' and with, of course, a cross-reference from 'Tyler' as from the other variants. Dr Hunnisett urges this on grounds of tidiness and consistency, but an even more cogent reason appears when we consider Tyler's relations. If we separate the rebel from the other Tilers and place him under Tyler, it would be absurd not to put his father there too – and his brother and his nephew and his cousins: where in the family do we draw the line? The only possible answer must be to do as Dr Hunnisett recommends and place them all under Tiler.

Place-names give the indexer fewer problems than personal names and there is only one point I would mention. Each one will presumably be identified with reference to a county or country: 'Deerhurst, *Gloucestershire*', 'Rouen, *France*', and so on. It is good practice to give cross-references to these from an entry for the county or country itself: 'Gloucestershire, *see* Deerhurst; Gloucester; Stroud', 'France, ... , *see also* Avignon; Bordeaux; Paris; Rouen'. This is immensely helpful to anyone looking for references to the area in question – it saves having to search the entire index for the relevant entries. In the Portsmouth series the peculiar topography of the area has led us to bring together in the same way cross-references for all places indexed in Portsea Island, and the inevitable maritime bias of the series has led us to devise conventions for names of coastal waters, their shoals and channels: we relate them to the relevant county – 'Nore, *coast of Kent*' – and include them in the cross-references listed under its name, as well as giving cross-references to all of them under the heading 'ships and shipping: seaways'. So far this has worked well, producing no serious problems; just as places may be in more than one county – 'Deptford, *Kent and*

7　　*ibid.*, p.43.

Surrey' – with cross-references from both, so too a maritime feature may lie off the coast of more than one, and the same system is used for rivers, though if they flow through more than two counties they are considered sufficiently important to stand on their own, without county identification or cross-reference – 'Enborne, River, *Berks. and Hants.*', but 'Thames, River' just thus.

Subjects

Indexing subjects raises many difficulties. When it came to compiling a subject index for my volume of Cuxham manorial records I allowed myself to be daunted by the size and complexity of the task and confined myself to an index of persons and places, sheltering behind the fig-leaf that the accounts that make up the bulk of the volume are so well ordered that an index of subjects would serve little purpose. This was sheer cowardice. I was wrong, and was rightly criticised by at least one reviewer. It is difficult to think of any records that do not need a subject index when they are published – certainly medieval manorial accounts are not among them. For lack of it the edition is effectively not available to some of those who might properly expect to make use of it.

A good case can be made for a separate index of subjects. It has the great advantage that a reader can run an eye over it and, because it contains none of the far more numerous names of persons and places, see at a glance how it is organised, whether one should look for gardens under 'gardens' or under 'houses' or 'land' or whatever. The trouble is that there are many ways of marshalling a subject index, none of them perfect – like the different projections of a globe as a map, each has its own advantages and drawbacks. It is easy enough to say that if gardens are mentioned in the text they should be indexed under 'gardens'. But suppose that in other passages it does not mention the word garden, but refers to a lawn, or a flower-bed, or a parterre, or a shrubbery – anyone interested in gardens would be interested in these too. Do we enter all these words separately, with a massive system of cross-references that can easily get entirely out of hand? Or do we put them all under 'gardens'? This introduces an element of artificial classification – and why stop there? Anyone interested in land usage will be interested in gardens: should the gardens themselves not be placed under 'land'? To take a different example, Mr T.R. Padfield, reviewing a Portsmouth volume, queried our placing 'treenail' (wooden dowel) under 'articles of utility' instead of in its proper alphabetical place.[8] Yes, perhaps, but if one was interested in wooden dowels, would one remember that they might be called treenails? If interested in nails of any kind, should one have to search under a whole range of possible headings – dowels, nails, sprigs, tacks, treenails and probably

8   *Archives*, no.81 (April 1989), p.43.

many more? Some element of classification is almost bound to be a component of any subject index, especially if its structure is designed not for a single volume but for a series; and with a separate subject index, which will be relatively short, this structure will become clearly apparent, so that one can see quite easily where one should look for gardens, whether nails are all grouped together and so on. In the last resort, without the names of persons and places, the subject index will be short enough to make it practicable to search it from beginning to end.

So much for the advantages of a separate subject index; the system can work well, as demonstrated by, say, the Wiltshire Record Society. But it has its disadvantages too. I came up against these recently when I was looking for references to manorial reeves in the twelfth century. If a reeve had no by-name beyond that of his office – Johannes Prepositus, that is John Reeve – he would appear in the index of persons and places, under Prepositus in some indexes, under Reeve in others. If, however, he was called Johannes de Sutton, *prepositus*, he would be placed under Sutton and could be found only through the index of subjects under 'reeves'; thus for a straight-forward enquiry two indexes would have to be searched, not one, whereas if the two indexes were combined all the entries would come together, under 'Reeve' and 'reeves' if the Latham-Hunnisett rules were followed. There will be many similar cases where cross-references from a subject to the names of places or persons are helpful – I have already mentioned the Portsmouth references from 'ships and ship-ping: seaways' to the names of individual waters, and others might be from a subject-heading 'castles' to the relevant places, or from 'Church: bishops' to the names of individual prelates, and so on. To have to refer, in all these cases, from one index to another is, to say the least, a clumsy device.

For these reasons I prefer a single index combining subjects with the names of persons and places. However, something must be done to reveal the structure of the subject entries, which at first sight will seem all but swamped by the surrounding entries of names. For the Portsmouth series I devised a system to meet this difficulty. This system is a sound one, but at the start I did not think through all its implications as fully as I should and have had to modify it in successive volumes. The notes at the start of each index include a list of the broad subject headings that occur in the index: antiquities, Army, articles of utility (this very useful heading was taken from the Public Record Office calendars), arts, buildings and grounds, and so on. These headings are unchanging throughout the series, though they do not all occur in every volume; the full list, of some thirty headings, is given here in Appendix 2. In each index there will be many other subject entries as well, but to every one there is a cross-reference from one or more of these broad subject headings. Thus 'corn' and 'wheat' have cross-references from both the broad subject headings 'flora' and 'food and drink', while there is also a cross-reference to 'wheat' from 'corn'. The cross-references need not be from the same broad headings each time; if the corn is being grown there will be one from 'industry and production' but if it is being exported there will be one from 'trade and commerce'.

The intention of the system is that one should be able to go directly to a particular subject, say wheat, without troubling with the note at the front or with the broad headings. If, however, one is interested in corn crops in general, looking up 'flora' will show at once what relevant entries there are in the index – 'barley', 'corn', 'wheat', for instance – or if one's interest is in corn as an aspect of food, 'food and drink' will give these same entries besides others – say 'bread', 'flour and meal' – that are also relevant in this context. Most readers will look up the subject entries while knowing nothing of the underlying system, but those who want to be sure they have found all entries relevant to a particular broader field can do so very easily, for a single volume or for throughout the series.

It was, I think, a correct decision to bring all ships' names together under a single heading, 'ships and shipping: ships named'. They are treated like the entries of persons' names: it is an index of names, not of ships, and there is no attempt to separate two ships of the same name, or to bring together the entries for a ship whose name was changed. The single list – which can run to well over a hundred entries – permits a rapid conspectus of all the ships named in a volume. I am less certain that it has been correct to bring together a single list of 'occupations' or to list all types of document under 'documents and diplomatic'; it would probably have been better to put 'butchers' and 'letters patent' at their proper places in the alphabet, which is where any reader will first look for them, with lists of cross-references under the broader headings providing the overview. And I am sure I was wrong to put a great many individual items under other broad headings in our early volumes. In the first volume, for instance, though I gave separate entries to 'beer and ale', 'bread', 'cheese', 'wine' and a few others, most entries for 'food and drink' – brandy, butter, fruit, herbs, meat, nuts, oil, salt, sugar and vegetables – were brought under this single heading. They should certainly have been spread throughout the index, with only cross-references here, and in subsequent volumes, heedless of my own injunctions against variation from one index to the next, I have gradually moved more and more items away from these broad subject headings and have given them individual entries with cross-references. Mr Padfield is right: the proper place for 'treenails' is in the full alphabetical sequence, with a cross-reference from 'articles of utility' and perhaps from 'shipbuilding' as well, and the proper form for the overview, the conspectus of the subject as a whole, is a series of cross-references under the broad headings. I believe the system is a sound and workable one, but I lacked the courage of my convictions when I began to put it into operation.

The minutiae of indexing evoke strong emotions among the users of published historical records – understandably, for they will nearly all have to use the index as their only gateway, their only means of access, to the text. Producing the index is one of the most important parts of the editor's job, and it is also one of the hardest, for it calls for a real effort of imagination, putting oneself in the shoes of someone who is coming to the text for the first time, and coming to it through the index. As Dr Hunnisett shrewdly observes, 'the indexer must never forget that, whereas he works from the text to the index, almost every user will work from the index to the text: an index is not primarily for the benefit of the few future indexers of cognate publications, but for the assistance of historians'.[9]

9   Hunnisett, *Indexing for Editors*, p.8.

Conclusion

The three rules for editing historical documents cannot be repeated too often:

1 Be accurate;
2 Say what you are going to do and do it;
3 Give full references to the document and describe it.

Nothing else matters – it is no more than style.

I shall be disappointed if my readers suppose this book has been written with a view to urging the particular points of style that I favour, that I want editors of historical records to expand all abbreviations with italics apart from a list for silent expansion, to have professionally designed layout, to give source references in the glossary, to combine subjects with persons and places in a single index, to follow all the other practices that I have said I like. Nothing could be further from my intention. It would be gratifying, of course, if everyone were to agree with me – but I shall not be worried in the least if they do not. What I have been trying to suggest is that these points of style have an importance all their own. They deserve careful thought and well integrated decisions, never mind what these decisions are.

Raising the profile of editing British historical records from the abyss into which it had fallen a century ago has now been proceeding, quietly and steadily, for many years. I hope the process will continue – even that this book may contribute to it. It is work important to the development of historical knowledge of every kind, work that demands the highest levels of scholarship, creativity, craftsmanship and, to use Joseph Hunter's words, 'due reverence for the actual text'. The skills it calls for are very like those needed for writing historical monographs, but directed, fascinatingly, to a different end with a different underlying philosophy. Editing historical records deserves still greater recognition, and therewith greater critical awareness of good and bad practice, in the universities and elsewhere. If I have helped to persuade any readers of this I shall be well satisfied.

But above all I shall be satisfied if the three rules come to be universally adopted as a *sine qua non* of record publication. Most editors observe them scrupulously – they are basic to the whole operation – but we still see the occasional lapse. The three rules are all that really matters.

Appendix 1:
List of Portsmouth Record Series

As it is published by a local authority (vols 1–7 by Portsmouth City Council, vols 8–11 by Hampshire County Council), the Series is omitted from E.L.C. Mullins, *Texts and Calendars II: an Analytical Guide to Serial Publications 1957–1982* (Royal Historical Society, Guides and Handbooks, 12; 1983). It is listed here:

1   Borough sessions papers 1653–1688. A calendar compiled by Arthur J. Willis and edited by Margaret J. Hoad with an introduction by Margaret J. Hoad and Robert P. Grime. 1971.

2   Portsmouth and Sheet turnpike commissioners' minute book 1711–1754. Edited by William Albert and P.D.A. Harvey. 1973.

3   Book of Original Entries 1731–1751. Edited by N.W. Surry and J.H. Thomas. 1976.

4   Maps of Portsmouth before 1801. A catalogue compiled by D. Hodson. 1978.

5   Records of university adult education 1886–1939. A calendar compiled by Edwin Welch. 1985.

6   Portsmouth Dockyard papers 1774–1783: the American war. A calendar compiled by R.J.B. Knight. 1987.

7   Records of the Portsmouth Division of Marines 1764–1800. Edited by J.A. Lowe. 1990.

8   Portsmouth Customs letter books 1748–1750. Edited by G. Hampson with an introduction by G. Hampson and J.G. Rule. 1994.

9   Portsmouth royal charters 1194–1974. Edited and translated by G.H. Martin. 1995.

10 Portsmouth Dockyard papers 1852–1869. A calendar compiled by C.I. Hamilton. 2001.

11 Portsmouth deeds before 1547. A calendar compiled by Katharine A. Hanna. 2002.

Appendix 2: List of main subject headings for index

The following is the full list of the main subject headings that have been used in the indexes of the Portsmouth Record Series; any other subject entry is linked to one or more of them by cross-reference (above, p.94).

administration, local
administration, national
administration, private
aliens
antiquities
Army
articles of utility
arts
buildings and grounds
Church, clergy and religion
documents and diplomatic
drainage
education
fauna
flora
folklore and customs
food and drink

games and entertainments
industry and production
land
languages
law and justice
medicine
natural phenomena
Navy
newspapers
periodicals
political activity
population
royal events
science and learning
trade and commerce
transport and communications
war and rebellion

Further works to consult

The art of editing literary texts has attracted a considerable literature; the art of editing records has not. Two works by R.F. Hunnisett in the British Records Association's Archives and the User series are an essential starting-point: *Editing Records for Publication* (no.4; 1977) and *Indexing for Editors* (no.2; 2nd edn, 1997). To these may be added 'Report on editing historical documents', *Bulletin of the Institute of Historical Research*, 1 (1923–4), pp. 6–25, and 'Report on editing modern historical documents', *ibid.*, 3 (1925–6), pp. 13–26. One record society that produced comprehensive guidance (no longer current) for its editors is the Hakluyt Society: *Guide for Editors of the Hakluyt Society's Publications* (2nd edn, 1975). General editorial guides to such matters as spelling and punctuation include *Hart's Rules for Compositors and Readers at the University Press Oxford* (39th edn, London, 1983) and J. Butcher, *Copy-Editing: the Cambridge Handbook for Editors, Authors and Publishers* (3rd edn, Cambridge, 1992).

Basic bibliographies of record publication by government bodies and private societies are three volumes in the Royal Historical Society's Guides and Handbooks series: E.L.C. Mullins, *Texts and Calendars: an Analytical Guide to Serial Publications* (no.7; 1958), with its supplement, E.L.C. Mullins, *Texts and Calendars II: an Analytical Guide to Serial Publications 1957–1982* (no.12; 1983), and, for Scottish societies, D. and W.B. Stevenson, *Scottish Texts and Calendars: an Analytical Guide to Serial Publications* (no.14; 1987), which was published also by the Scottish History Society, 4th series, vol.23. *Texts and Calendars* is brought up to date on the Historical Manuscripts Commission's website <http://www.hmc.gov.uk>. These bibliographies do not include works published commercially or other individual publications, which have mostly been personal records such as letters and diaries, nor do they include the many texts published by local authorities, among them the important series of calendars of the City of London's records. *Surveys of Historical Manuscripts in the United Kingdom: a Select Bibliography* (Historical Manuscripts Commission; 3rd edn 1997) is an invaluable starting-point for discovering what records exist and which have been published.

Index